OLD BEFORE MY TIME

HAYLEY and KERRY OKINES

with ALISON STOKES

Published by Accent Press Ltd – 2011

First Impression November 2011
Second Impression November 2011
Third Impression December 2011

ISBN 9781908192554

Printed and bound in the UK by CPI Group (UK) Ltd, Croydon, CR0 4YY

Cover design by Madamadari

Hayley's Dedication

I WOULD LIKE TO say a huge thank you to my Mum and Dad for always being there for me. You have put up with travelling, hospital visits and with me and my attitude. I love you both so much.

Thank you for taking me to the most amazing places all over the world. Thank you so much, love from your daughter Hayley.

A massive massive thank you to my special Pops and Nanna, family and friends.

A special thanks to Erin for being my best friend for the past 10 years. You have seen me laugh, cry, and have been there to lift my spirits when things get me down.

Thank you to James and Nicki from Rabbit Productions for taking their time to capture parts of my life. I know I was probably a pain sometimes but it was so worth it.

I love and miss my dearest friend, who unfortunately passed away 5 years ago. Life is not the same without you here. I wish I could just have 5 more minutes with you to tell you just how much you mean to me.

Hayley xxx

Kerry's Dedication

THANKS TO MY MUM, dad and family for being my rock, giving me support and your unconditional love through the good times and bad.

Thank you to my friends, ones that have come and gone and ones that have stayed by my side.

Thanks to Rabbit productions – Nicki and James – for helping us with our quest to raise awareness and for making Hayley a star.

Thanks to all the doctors and scientist who are working extremely hard in finding a cure for Progeria.

A big thanks to Dr Graham Whincup, not only for being Hayley's favourite doctor but also becoming a family friend.

Thanks to Dr Sheila Mohammed for your help in the very early days of Hayley's diagnosis.

Dr Lorna Bray for your care and support after Hayley's diagnosis.

Mr Hinves for the special and delicate care you have given and continue to give Hayley throughout her dislocations.

A big thank you to Hayley for being my daughter, my friend, someone to laugh with and cry with. Thank you for all the special memories you have given me.
Love you lots and always.

Kerry

Introduction

MY NAME IS HAYLEY Okines and people tell me I am special.

I have a disease called Hutchinson-Gilford Progeria that makes me age eight times faster than other people.

The easiest way to explain it is it's like my body is a hundred years old when I am actually thirteen, but I don't like it when people call me old because I don't feel like I am a hundred years old.

I am smaller than other kids my age. I have a brother, Louis, who is nine and a sister, Ruby, who is six. Although I am the big sister in the family they are actually bigger than me.

Mum says I am one in eight million because my condition is so rare. I have had lots of TV programmes made about me because I am so different, and people I don't know come up to me and say, 'Hi, have I seen you on the telly?' and I have to smile and be polite.

Living with progeria is hard because people treat you like a baby. The worst is having all the treatment and needles. I have been going to America for special treatment that we hope will cure my progeria. I know the new drugs will not make me look like other kids but they will help me to grow hair and live longer.

Sometimes people ask me if I could have three wishes would I wish I didn't have progeria. And I say no. It would be good to not have it, and it would be fun to go out and not get stared at and not have loads of people ask questions. I would rather have progeria than not have it, though. Don't ask me why, but I wouldn't change it.

When Mum and Dad first found out I had progeria the doctors said I would only live to thirteen.

On December 3 2011, I will be fourteen.

I am not worried about dying. They said the Titanic wouldn't sink but it did, so that proves experts can be wrong and I want to prove the doctors wrong.

My life with progeria is full of happiness and good memories. If I didn't have progeria I would not have done most of the cool things I have done or met most of the cool people I have met.

Deep inside I am no different from anyone. We are all human.

Chapter 1
Kerry
We're Having a Baby

TWO LINES APPEARED IN the window. 'What the hell am I going to tell Mark? He's going to hit the roof,' I said to my friend and confidante, Jane. It was the fourth pregnancy test stick I had peed on in three days and the results were the same. I was pregnant.

I could feel the butterflies starting to flutter in my stomach just thinking of the conversation that lay ahead when my boyfriend came home from work. Thirteen years older than me, Mark was already a single dad to Stacey, seven, and Charlotte, twelve, from his previous marriage, so his nappy-changing years were behind him. We had only been dating for a couple of months and I thought I had been safe on the contraceptive pill. Despite the initial shock I was thrilled at the thought of being a first-time mum. It was all I had ever wanted. My first Christmas memory when I was a kid was the year my dad had made two blue, wooden cots for me and my sister Janie. I must have only been three, Janie was two, and we played with those cots for years, pretending to be mums to our rag dolls. We would carry them everywhere, feeding them and changing nappies.

Now I was twenty-four and my life would soon be complete.

I could never understand those career women who would sacrifice everything for their work. I would happily have given up my job in the school kitchen just to have a baby to love and care for. I thought there was nothing like the love between a mother and child, it was unconditional and everlasting and something I wanted. After years of dating boys who were afraid of commitment, I wanted someone to love me as much as I loved him or her; and a baby would give me that love I craved.

'Maybe I should hang a pair of baby booties on the front door knocker. Perhaps that will give him a hint,' I joked with Jane, thinking of ways I could soften the blow.

When Mark arrived home that evening after his 12-hour shift at the parcel delivery company, I was sitting on the sofa alone watching *Emmerdale*. The four positive pregnancy tests were laid out on the cushion next to me.

As he took off his coat and hung it on the back of the chair he noticed the plastic sticks on the sofa.

'We're having a baby,' I chirped before he had the chance to say anything.

'Are you sure?' From the look on his face anyone would have thought I had slapped him with a month-old kipper.

'Of course I am. I've got an appointment with the doctor on Friday. But that will only confirm what I already know. We're going to be parents.' As I had expected, the reaction was not good. The silent treatment lasted for days as Mark sulked over the news of the addition to his family.

Looking back, I can understand Mark's less than ecstatic reaction. It was all happening too quickly.

Perhaps we should have been more careful. I was probably too young to be part of a ready-made family with another baby on the way. But I didn't consider that at the time. I had grown up in a large family. In my immediate family I was the eldest of three. My sister was only a year younger than me. When I was just three months old my mum had one hell of a shock when she took me for a check up at the baby clinic and discovered she was expecting Janie. My half-brother, Steven, was six years younger. My mother was one of seven and my dad was one of 11, so Christmases and special occasions were always big events.

Mark, on the other hand, had come from a small family. His mother, Brigitte, and her sister fled from East Germany as the partition of Berlin was beginning in 1951. After settling in Hastings, she met Mark's dad who was driving the trams. He had one younger sister and no nieces and nephews, so he was used to the quiet life.

Mark also had a good reason to be fearful of another baby. He and his ex-wife Jane, who was also my best friend, had lost their second daughter, Lucy, to cot death when she was just eight weeks old. The trauma of trying to give his tiny baby the kiss of life had haunted him for years and quite understandably he was worried that it would happen all over again. All of this was a perfectly acceptable reaction to the baby news, but, being a typical bloke, he didn't share his feelings with me. He just sulked.

The reality hit when I came back from my first ultrasound scan with a blurry black and white photo of our healthy baby girl and a due date of November 30 1997. Mark started coming round to the idea of the new addition and for the next few months we enjoyed our final period of freedom knowing our carefree days would soon be over.

We both loved dance music and clubbing. That's how we met. I was working as a shelf-stacker at Somerfield supermarket with Mark's ex-wife near my parents' home in Cranbrook, Kent. One afternoon as she was filling up her freezer section with fish fingers and I was rotating the full-fat milk in my fridge area, she said, 'Me and Mark and a few friends are going to the Eighties Night at Saturdays nightclub in Hastings this weekend. Fancy joining us?' Why not? I thought, I'm footloose and fancy free.

Duran Duran's 'Rio' was playing as we hit the club. 'C'mon. Let's dance,' said Jane, dragging me on to the crowded disco floor. If I'm totally honest, eighties pop music wasn't really my bag, I was more of a trance and house music fan. I was having fun, though. As Duran Duran segued into Kylie Minogue we were really warming up to the music. Then I noticed Jane gesticulating to a bloke with a greying goatee beard who was standing by the bar.

'Who are you chasing?' I shouted to be heard above the disco beat.

'That's my ex, Mark.' I had heard Jane talk of her ex-husband and her two daughters and I had always been impressed by how they managed to stay good friends after their divorce. What I didn't realise was that she was playing match-maker.

'Can I get you a drink?' Mark asked once we had finally fought our way from the dance floor to the bar.

'I'll have a vodka with lime and lemonade – no ice,' I replied, not realising that this was his attempt at a chat-up line.

Drinks in hand, we talked about work and music. Mark and I had more in common than I imagined. We shared the same taste in music and the same dry sense of humour. But there was zero chemistry. I just thought he seemed like a nice bloke. As the weeks passed, I went out more with Jane, and Mark would always be there too. Call me stupid but I didn't think anything of it – a bunch of girls and one bloke who always seemed to make a beeline to talk to me. I

4

didn't even realise that he had made a special effort and combed his hair, which was dark brown, cropped short and peppered with a hint of grey. Mark was just another friend. That was until Christmas when I invited Mark to a party.

'You can stay at my place if you don't want to get a taxi home,' he offered. So I did. Two weeks later I had virtually moved in. And the rest, as they say, is history.

It turned out Mark was a bit of mix master. He had a set of DJ decks at his house and he would make me mixtapes, which were as good as anything I'd heard played at the clubs. Mark also introduced me to the rave scene. In those days – the late 90s – illegal raves were still popular and the Kent countryside across the border from our home in Sussex was a prime location. It was always a game of cat and mouse, the ravers versus the police and authorities. Under the darkness of the night we would drop Mark's daughters off at the babysitters and drive out into the countryside, following an anonymous tip-off and a convoy of headlights into the countryside until we arrived at a field where there was a party in full swing. We would dance non-stop, my favourite tune at the time was 'Take Me Away', by a band called 4 Strings, a really uplifting dance anthem that always got me waving my glow sticks in the air. When the sun rose over the hedges we would head home, relieved that the police and council officials had not raided the party. Once I had a taste for the great outdoors, Mark introduced me to festivals like Global Gathering and Cream Fields, three days of non-stop dancing. I was in my element.

After a hedonistic summer of festivals and fun, Mark and I started preparing for our new arrival.

We were living in a two-bedroom council house on an

estate in the sleepy seaside town of Bexhill-on-Sea on the East Sussex coast. Space was at a premium. We had no room for a nursery and money was tight. I had changed jobs and was working as a chambermaid at a local hotel while Mark was working up to 12-hour shifts at the local Amtrak parcel delivery company just to make ends meet. He always said to me, 'Don't worry about money,' which I later realised meant we never had any money so we had no worries. With two children to care for and a third on the way there was never any spare cash for luxuries at the end of the month. We begged and borrowed to collect what we needed for our new arrival. My mum had bought us a second-hand pram, a friend gave us a cot and I had found a used Moses basket for sale in the small ads of our local newspaper. It was all set up in our bedroom ready for the new arrival.

At 3 a.m. on Monday December 1 1997 I was woken up by an agonising labour pain in my tummy.

'She's coming,' I shouted to Mark as I reached for the TENS machine and attached the electrode to my spine to ease the pain.

'I think you'd better stay home from work.' I winced as another pain shot through my body. I was two days past my due date and although it was my first child I was sure it wasn't a false alarm.

Throughout the day I counted the seconds between the contractions as they got shorter. I ran myself a hot bath to ease the discomfort. At 7 p.m. – just as we were sitting down to a takeaway kebab – the contractions changed.

'I think it's time for hospital.' Mark helped me into the back of his red Ford Sierra and drove me five miles to the maternity unit at Hastings Conquest Hospital.

I will never forget the moment – 2.50 p.m. on

Wednesday December 3 – when Rita the midwife laid my baby on my tummy. Just days before I had gone into labour I had a dream about our baby. I imagined I was being handed a bundle of blankets and all I could see was one big blue eye, nothing else. Now as I looked down, my head still drifting away on the large doses of gas and air, I saw just one eye, bright blue and sparkling like an aquamarine gem, looking up at me. It lit up the room. She reached out to touch the air with her perfect little fingers and I immediately felt relief. The pain was over. Our little girl was healthy.

I looked at Mark, who had stayed by my side throughout the entire delivery and said, 'Don't it look like she's got highlights?' Her head was plastered with a thick mop of brown hair.

'Hello, Hayley,' Mark whispered. We had already decided we would name her after the comet Hale Bopp, which had been streaking across the sky on the night that she was conceived.

She was absolutely beautiful. Weighing in at 6lb 6oz, she was perfect. As we cooed over her, a smile broke out across her elfin face. It was the first of many.

'She's gonna be a cheeky one,' Mark warned, 'she's got your wicked glint in her eye.'

I would have punched him playfully but I didn't have the energy. After a 40-hour labour I was knackered but I was also the happiest woman in the world.

Chapter 2
Kerry
Am I Being Paranoid?

I WAS ON A permanent high for weeks after Hayley was born. Mark and I moved into a new phase in our relationship, taking on the role of new parents. Charlotte and Stacey were thrilled to have a little half-sister to care for and would help me to change her nappy and nurse her to sleep.

Some new mums always complain of being tired, but not me. I seemed to have more energy than I had ever had before and I had lots of support from my family, who were equally besotted with our new addition to the family.

Late one night, just as we were settling down for bed, there was a knock on the front door. We were not expecting visitors so late in the night. When I opened the door, my mum was standing there. 'I just had to see her again,' she said, having made a 90-minute trip from her home in Kent. Little Hayley had cast a magical spell over us all.

Hayley was what the midwife called a 'grazer', which meant she would eat little and often. As I was breastfeeding it meant I was getting up every two or three hours during the night to feed her. But I didn't mind. As the weeks passed, I started to worry that Hayley was not gaining weight. She could still fit into the little makeshift gown that she had been dressed in when she was born because she was too small to wear the hospital-issue baby-grow.

Every week I would take her to the baby clinic and every week there was little change. When the health visitor lifted her on to the scales she looked like a plucked chicken with her bony legs dangling from her chubby little body, but the scales hardly moved no matter how much she ate. Being a first-time mother I had bought all of the 'new mum' books I could, and I followed the baby growth chart religiously. By my reckoning Hayley should have been gaining a pound or two every session, but she was only registering an ounce or two. Instead of a healthy arc, Hayley's growth seemed to be flat-lining. I started to dread our appointments at the clinic. I was feeling paranoid. What if the nurses thought I was neglecting our child?

'Maybe I'm feeding her wrong,' I moaned to my mum, who assured me that I was doing everything by the book. Soon I switched to feeding her baby formula milk, after my health visitor suggested my own milk might not be rich enough. But even that did little to tip the scales.

One morning as I was changing her nappy I noticed she had two little lumps either side of her belly button. 'It looks like she's got a hernia or something,' my mum suggested. I made an appointment with my local GP, but he dismissed it as 'nothing to worry about'. I got the feeling that they thought I was being an over-protective first-time mother, that it seemed like I wasn't satisfied with a healthy, happy baby and I was looking for trouble. But I couldn't ignore the fact that Hayley was very small for her age.

By the time she was six months old, Mark and I had convinced ourselves that something was seriously wrong.

She was still wearing newborn baby nappies and clothes for a 0–3-month-old. But the doctors still didn't share our worries. I was beginning to think perhaps I was being paranoid. By her first birthday the doctors started to show concern too. Hayley was still pitifully underweight. The lumps next to her belly button were still visible and the skin around her tummy was tight and thin, almost as if there was cling-film wrapped around her. Call it a mother's intuition, but I knew there was something not quite right. Eventually my GP agreed to refer us to a consultant at London's Guy's Hospital.

Over the following months Hayley had test after test. Every couple of weeks Mark and I would take Hayley on the 150-mile round trip from our home in Bexhill to the centre of London for our appointments. At first Hayley thought it was a big adventure, she would sit on the train with her colouring and counting books. Over the months she became a human pin-cushion as samples of her blood were sucked out of her and sent off for analysis. They even tested her chromosomes, but they could not find anything to cause concern. At one stage they thought she might be suffering from cystic fibrosis. At that point an alarm bell rang in my head as I remembered a boy who lived in our street and suffered from the condition. We were told he would be lucky to see his 14th birthday as there was no cure for cystic fibrosis. I always remembered how he struggled to breathe and was continually coughing up thick green mucus from his lungs. Being a school-kid at the time I recall I found this particularly disgusting. The doctors told us that cystic fibrosis was not uncommon in children and on average five babies a week were born with it. It was terrifying to think that Hayley could be suffering from a life-threatening illness. I thought she might never live to reach her twenties and would spend most of her young life struggling for breath, and having to go through a daily regime of physiotherapy to clear away the mucus that would clog up her lungs.

When the results for the cystic fibrosis test came back negative I thought, Phew! At least we don't have to deal with that. With this ruled out, Mark and I had a new glimmer of hope. We were referred to specialists at Great Ormond Street Hospital. At the time it did not register just how serious the situation could be. Over the years I had watched enough documentaries following the work of the Hospital for Sick Children, its young patients and its groundbreaking research into serious and unusual illnesses to know that it was one of the best children's hospitals in the world. Mark and I hoped its specialist doctors would be able to give us the answers we needed and treat whatever was stunting Hayley's growth so we could get on with our lives.

At Great Ormond Street we were referred to the department headed by the late Professor Robin Winter, a clinical geneticist whose field of expertise was dysmorphology (using a patient's outward appearance to diagnose rare and unusual genetic syndromes). His colleague Dr Sheila Mohammed, an Asian lady with an air of calm about her, arranged a skin and hair biopsy. Taking a sample of hair was easy, but the tests required that they cut a piece of skin from Hayley's left arm. She was given an injection to numb her arm. I think this was probably the start of her phobia about needles. What followed next was too awful to watch. Hayley sat on my lap as Dr Mohammed brought her scalpel up close to Hayley's arm to shave off a sample of skin. Hayley screamed and squirmed trying to get away from the scalpel. I was powerless. I knew it was something that had to be done but I couldn't stand to watch. Eventually I had to stand outside the doctor's room as three nurses held her still so Dr Mohammed could take a sample.

'We think Hayley may have a rare genetic condition called Hutchinson-Gilford Progeria,' Dr Mohammed said at our next consultation when the results of the skin biopsy came back. 'Her skin has an alarming lack of elasticity for a child so young.' Writing the word progeria on a page torn out of her notepad, she told us to go home and do some research.

'We can't be certain at this stage. We are still waiting for some of the tests from her skin biopsy. But we could be looking at a rare ageing disorder.' As we left the consulting room, knowing it would be two weeks before our next meeting, Dr Mohammed warned us, 'Be very careful what you read about progeria. Not everything on the internet is factual.'

On the car journey home, Mark and I looked at each other baffled.

'Pro-jee-ree-ya?' I said, carefully spelling out every syllable. 'I love watching medical documentaries on the telly, and I've never heard of that one before.'

'It sounds like something from a science fiction film,' he suggested. All the way home we wondered what this ageing disorder could mean. What did it matter if Hayley's skin wasn't as springy as other toddlers? I pinched the back of my hand and watched my own skin snap back into place. I reached out to touch my baby girl, who was strapped into her car seat watching the world fly by through the car window. Now the thought had been put in my mind, her skin did seem different.

But did it really matter? At almost two years old Hayley was already the centre of our world. She was smaller than other toddlers in play group but what she lacked in size she made up for in intelligence. She was

13

advanced for her age. She had taken her first steps at 10 months old. By the time she was 18 months you could hold conversations with her. She knew the colours of the rainbow and could count to 10. She definitely seemed much wiser and more inquisitive than other 20-month-old toddlers.

When we got home we shot around to see our friend Andy who was the only person we knew who owned a home computer. We tapped the word progeria into the Ask Jeeves search engine, taking care to spell it as the doctor had written it down. Then we waited as the results started to appear on our screens. One by one photos of children who looked like little old people, flashed up on the monitor. There was one little girl with arms so thin, you could see her bony elbows through her skin. Her face was ancient and shrivelled. She looked like she was a hundred years old. She was just 12. And she had passed away.

On another page there was an image of a little boy with a large bulbous bald head, laced with blue veins, and eyes as wide as a bush baby.

We learnt that Hutchinson-Gilford Progeria Syndrome is a very rare disorder characterized by children ageing eight times faster than normal. The word progeria comes from the Greek, meaning prematurely old. Children with the condition experience growth delays in the first year of their life resulting in short stature and low weight. That could explain why Hayley was still low on her growth chart. The website described how children with progeria suffer from deterioration of the layer of fat beneath their skin. Characteristics of the syndrome were abnormally small faces, underdeveloped jaws, unusually prominent eyes, and sometimes small 'beak-like' noses.

I stared at Hayley, who was asleep in her Moses basket, looking for these abnormalities that made the children look so strange and space-like. But she didn't look like them. Yes she had big eyes, but so did I when I was her age. The website said that in the first year or two of their life Progeria children's scalp hair, eyebrows, and eyelashes may become sparse, and veins of the scalp may become unusually prominent. Hayley's hair was thick, tied up in her pretty pink headband, she looked like she had a fine head of highlights.

As we read on we were horrified to discover that not only did these children look like old people, but they suffered the same ageing illnesses too: arthritis and joint stiffness, bones that broke easily and would not heal properly, ageing skin, tooth problems, and heart problems.

But the words that really hit us hard were: *Children with progeria die of heart disease or strokes at an average age of thirteen years.*

'The doctors must be wrong. Hayley doesn't look like those children. Turn it off,' I screamed reaching for the switch to power off the computer. I didn't want to know any more. The thought that our beautiful daughter would not live long enough to become a troublesome teenager was more than I could take. We thought that this was every parent's worst nightmare – knowing that our dear daughter would not make it to adulthood. I would never worry whether her first boyfriend would be good enough for her. Mark would never walk her down the aisle. My ambition had been to have a family of my own, but I wanted one for keeps. I couldn't face the thought that Hayley might be snatched away from us as suddenly as she had come into our lives.

Chapter 3
Kerry
Progeria Confirmed

SEPTEMBER 30 1999 IS the day when I lost all hope that we would ever be a happy family again, when the 'maybe nots' and 'everything will be all rights' turned into 'sorrys'. For Mark and I the two weeks waiting for our next appointment with Dr Mohammed at Great Ormond Street Hospital moved in slow motion. It felt like we were waiting for a death sentence to be passed on our little Hayley. We were stuck in no man's land, scared at what our next visit to Great Ormond Street might bring, but daring to hope that some of the most senior specialists in the world might be wrong.

'It will be all right,' my mum said optimistically. 'Don't worry it won't be that,' Mark's mum reassured us. These sentiments were echoed by all our friends and family as the day of our appointment drew nearer.

'We've got more chance of winning the lottery than of Hayley having progeria,' Mark mused when he found a statistic on the internet that said it affected one in eight million children. I knew what I would rather. No contest.

The morning of the consultation, Hayley was her usual chirpy self. It was a crisp autumn morning as we left the house for our train journey to London. I had wrapped Hayley in her favourite pink leggings and padded pink anorak with fur around the hood. She looked like a cute little piece of candy floss and I wanted to eat her. While we sat in the waiting room, Hayley lay on the floor drawing.

'Look, Mummy, a 'pider,' she said handing me a red scribble on a scrap of paper. She had not yet grasped the word spider.

'That's a nice 'pider,' I replied as Dr Mohammed called our names.

The wait was over.

After that everything became a blur. I barely remember walking into the doctor's room, or registering the apologetic look on her face as she tried to explain how Hayley was 'a very special little girl. One in eight million.' It was confirmed she had Hutchinson-Gilford Progeria Syndrome, a genetic condition so rare that there were only 40 other known cases around the world and only one other child in the UK. It meant her body would age eight times faster than that of a normal human.

'What's the prognosis?' I asked. To this day I still do not know why I asked that question. I didn't even realise I knew such long words and I was certainly not prepared for the reply.

'The life expectancy is 13.'

At that point I collapsed on the floor, like someone had just pulled the carpet from under my feet. That was one piece of information from the internet that was correct.

On our way back to the train station in the back of a London cab, Mark and I sat in stunned silence. It was all too much to take in. There was so much we wanted to know, but couldn't find the words to ask. Dr Mohammed accompanied us on the taxi ride and as we parted company she gave us her home telephone number and told us to call any time.

'I want to see my mum,' was all I could say to Mark.

Suddenly I felt like I was three years old again and I wanted my mummy to make things better. Hayley sensed there was something wrong. She sat completely still on my lap throughout the entire journey, rubbing my face and kissing my cheek. It was all I could do to choke back the tears, struggling to make sense of an illness that was so rare only one other child in the country was known to have it. To make matters worse there were no other parents to talk to about it, no support groups or other sufferers for Hayley to meet. We felt completely alone on the start of a journey that would have no happy ending.

When we reached my parents' house, Dad was in the garden and Mum was in the kitchen. I was unable to speak. I just cried. There was nothing to say. Hayley ran out on to the lawn to see her 'Pops' while my mother put the kettle on. As we sat at the breakfast bar, the silence broken only by my sobs, I looked out of the window and saw Dad standing by the fishpond. He was holding Hayley's hand and pointing down to the fishies in the water to disguise the tears that were rolling down his cheek.

They say that before you can pick yourself up, you have to hit rock bottom. For Mark and I, the months that followed saw us freefalling into the darkest of places. Most nights, once Charlotte and Stacey were fast asleep and Hayley was tucked up in her cot at the foot of our bed, Mark and I would lie awake till 3 a.m. asking, 'Why Us? Why are we being punished?' We had been honest and open with Charlotte and Stacey, who were now thirteen and eight – old enough to be told the truth. But we tried our best to hide the full force of our grief from them. It was as if Hayley was living under the threat of execution. We knew it would happen, we just didn't know when. It could be tomorrow, it could be next week or it could be 10 years away, and that was the hardest thing to deal with. We had been hoping to be told Hayley had a rare condition and given a prescription for tablets to make it all better. But there was no cure and at that point it seemed there was no hope.

It put huge stress on my relationship with Mark – we were so distressed that we took it out on each other. At night when the girls were tucked up in bed we would fight over anything and everything. Who had drunk the last of the milk? Why had Mark left his jacket on the sofa? Why hadn't I washed the dishes? They were all trivial things that seemed so irrelevant in the bigger scheme of things. Sometimes Mark would come home late and I would yell at him, 'Where have you been?'

'I've been on Andy's computer. Finding out about progeria,' he would reply.

'Don't know why you're bothering. There's no cure,' I would snap back in frustration.

'But knowledge is power,' he would always say. At the time I thought it was just another way to annoy me, but he believed the more we understood the brighter the future. I was reacting differently. I couldn't see past the next day without Hayley.

One morning, after another argument, Mark had gone to work in a bad mood. He kissed Hayley goodbye and said nothing to me. Grabbing his coat from the hallway, he was gone. As I heard the door slam shut, I lay in bed and decided I would take action. I would end it all.

For some time after the diagnosis, I had been harbouring thoughts of death. If my baby could never live a long and healthy life, then why should I? I was burdened with the guilt that I had planted this ticking time bomb inside Hayley and I was the one who should be punished. We would go together. I had it all mapped out in my head. I had rationalised the best method, nothing messy. Pills. That would be easy. A bottle of vodka and a handful of paracetamol. Goodbye, Kerry. I rummaged around the bathroom cabinets looking for any tablets I could lay my hands on. A half-empty bottle of aspirin we kept for Stacey and Charlotte, a full bottle of paracetamol which I always used for headaches and a packet of ibuprofen painkillers which Mark sometimes took for aches and pains. I laid them all out on our bed and counted them. I had no idea whether the collection of over-the-counter drugs would be enough to end it all. As I summoned the courage to take the first one, I fought back my tears. I couldn't go through with it. I couldn't force-feed Hayley, who was just a baby, a lethal cocktail.

When Mark came home from work that evening I told him how close I had been to taking both of our lives. I don't think he realised how deep my sorrow was and made the decision to give up work to care for me. Although I didn't know it at the time, I was suffering from depression. I felt I had to keep everything together. I was living one day at a time, expecting each day to be Hayley's last. The burden was overpowering, but I couldn't share it with Mark for fear of upsetting him. I had to put on a brave face and soldier on when inside all I wanted to do was die.

Even with Mark to share my burden, the suicidal thoughts would not go away. I planned another suicide. While Hayley was still asleep I lay in our bed mapping out our final exit. We had a hosepipe in the garden shed. I could use that. Our Ford Sierra was parked on the drive. Once the girls had gone to school, I would get up, strap Hayley into her car seat and tell her we were going for a day trip. Then I would drive us out to Beachy Head, where it would be quiet. Once there, I could feed a hosepipe from the exhaust in through the window. I would have my Cafe del Mar compilation CD playing in the car and I would sit there and talk to Hayley as we drifted off into a painless future. It would be a release for both of us.

The sound of Hayley stirring awake in her cot suddenly brought me back to reality. As I bent over to pick her up, she looked at me with those big blue eyes and smiled. She looked so happy in her innocent ignorance. 'What on earth are you thinking, Kerry Button?' a voice inside my head, shouted. 'How could you even think of denying this child her happiness?'

That was the point of my breakdown. I called my mum in tears and sobbed down the phone, 'I don't want to live any more.'

She came to collect me and take me and Hayley back to Kent, there she and my dad mounted a round-the-clock suicide watch. But it was unnecessary. The doctor prescribed anti-depressants and Mum and Dad gave me the support I needed. I had sunk as low as I could go.

Chapter 4
Kerry
Learning to Live with Progeria

THE TURNING POINT IN my acceptance of Hayley's progeria came from conversations with other families who had already been through diagnosis and were not only coping, but living full and happy lives.

For the first few months after my breakdown I had been in complete denial, foolishly thinking that if I didn't acknowledge the progeria it would go away. Meanwhile in the background Mum and Mark were finding out more about the disease, driven on by Mark's mantra 'knowledge is power'. The world was still a big place in those days and with the few progeria families spread around the world, information for newly diagnosed children and their parents was like searching for that elusive needle in a haystack. Back then Google was still only a small private American company set up by two Stanford University students rather than a globally-recognised verb for finding information online. When we Asked Jeeves about progeria only 2,200 web pages appeared and many of those lacked hard information and facts. Whereas now you can sift through around two million pages on the condition and Hayley has more than 94,000 online references in addition to her dedicated progeria website. Even the UK's top doctors knew very little about the condition back then. Professor Winter at Great Ormond Street Hospital had only ever known of one other case in his career, so we were very much in the dark and finding help was mainly through word of mouth.

My mother was determined to track someone down who could help lift my depression. She spent hours on the phone talking to families and friends.

'I've just been speaking to a woman called Doreen in Northampton whose adopted son, Danny, had progeria,' she said after putting the phone down one day.

'Had,' I said, picking up on the past tense.

'Yes. He had classic progeria and he was 22 when he died in 1996. He's the longest survivor we know about, so there is some hope out there. Doreen helps families with children with progeria like you and she's expecting a call from you.'

My initial reaction was 'I can't' and I threw the piece of paper with Doreen's phone number in the bin. I didn't think anyone could help Hayley and couldn't see the point of wasting my breath or the cost of a telephone call.

On my doctor's advice Mark and I started seeing a counsellor at a local hospital to help us talk through our worries.

'What are your worst fears, Kerry?' my counsellor asked.

'No mother should bury her own daughter,' I whispered. Although physically and emotionally draining, the sessions allowed me to share my concerns. Voicing my inner demons gave me the strength to accept Hayley's progeria and move forward for everyone. When I finally felt strong enough to pick up the phone to call Doreen it was like a weight had been lifted off my shoulders.

Mum had been right all along. Just talking to someone

who had been at the point Mark and I were at helped. She understood my feelings and could relate to us. Speaking to her, I felt her positivity rub off on me. Even though she had lost her son, she talked about the happy times they had together and the joy of having a special child with progeria. She also told me about something called the Sunshine Progeria Reunion where all the known progeria children in the world and their families would meet in the United States for an annual get-together. She had taken her son for many years during his life and had continued to attend as a volunteer after his death. She also gave me a telephone number for a couple of doctors in America who had set up a new organisation called the Progeria Research Foundation to help families like Mark and me with information about the disease. Doreen's parting words were, 'Don't waste your time worrying about what might be. Make every minute count for Hayley.'

As part of our fact-finding mission we spoke to scientists to get a clearer understanding of what had gone wrong in Hayley's genes and attempted to find out whether it was genetic or just bad luck. We spoke to Dr Richard Faragher, a Research Scientist at the University of Brighton. He told us that progeria was a premature ageing disease, which mimics or caricatures many aspects of the normal ageing process.

'What you are seeing in all probability is the result of a gene that has just gone bad by accident in one or other of the parents. Any patient that has progeria is not very likely to live to produce children so the gene is unlikely to be passed down.'

I also called Dr Leslie Gordon, a very helpful mum in America. Leslie and her husband Scott Berns, both paediatricians, had a three-year-old son Sam who was diagnosed with Hutchinson-Gilford Progeria when he was

22 months old. They were a year ahead of us in their diagnosis but Leslie told me how difficult it had been even for a pair of doctors to find information. They had just started an organisation called the Progeria Research Foundation to help other families.

'We found there wasn't much available for families like us and there was no way to definitively test for the disease, no funding for progeria research, and no organisation advocating for children with progeria, so we are going to change that with our foundation. We are on a mission to find the cause in order to work on a treatment and cure,' she promised.

'We use the words 'premature ageing' in quotes because even though there are some aspects of ageing progeria children do have like wrinkled skin, hair loss and heart problems, their brains remain sharp and they are bright, sweet little children,' Dr Gordon said. Like us, the Gordons were on a sharp learning curve and determined to spread their knowledge with others.

Meanwhile life for Hayley went on. We made three-monthly visits to our nearest hospital – the Conquest Hospital, Hastings – for check-ups with consultant paediatrician Dr Lorna Bray. Although there was no medicine Hayley could take to cure the progeria, there was a cocktail of preventative pills and remedies to help her quality of life. One of the main concerns was that children with progeria usually died of heart attacks or strokes, just like old people. As a result our bathroom cabinet started to resemble that of a typical octogenarian. Her daily routine involved a concoction of pills, which we would joke made her rattle. Hayley has always been good at taking tablets, which was fortunate as she needed four doses of vitamin E with her meals to help her heart, cod liver oil for her joints and fluoride for her teeth. We learnt that most progeria children had problems with their teeth due to having underdeveloped facial bones and lower jaws, which meant that their teeth were slow to break through their gums and when they eventually did they were small and irregularly formed. Tooth decay was also a common problem so fluoride would help by strengthening her tooth enamel and making it more resistant to decay. We gave Hayley half of a 1.1mg tablet every day.

Narrowed coronary arteries was another common problem with progeria children and clinical trials had proved that a small daily dose of aspirin, enough to prevent dangerous blood clotting, reduced the risk of strokes and heart attacks. We started out by giving Hayley half of a 75mg tablet every day, but later reduced it to a quarter as we found her skin was bruising easily, one of the common side-effects. Hayley's eating problems which had started in her first months of life continued as she grew older, again we discovered that this was not uncommon in children with progeria, who had tiny stomachs. Throughout her life Hayley has never really enjoyed eating as she complains she gets full quickly. During her early years before bed-time we would give her a bottle of build-up milk called Nutrini which provided all of the nutrients essential for well-being and health. We later discovered something called Pro-Cal, which we would sprinkle into her morning cup of tea to add extra energy, protein and minerals to her diet.

Hayley's favourite item on Dr Bray's prescription was hydrotherapy. She didn't see it as medical – it was a chance to put on her pink water wings and matching pink costume and go swimming. From an early age Mark took her to our local hospital for 30-minute sessions in the hydrotherapy pool. It helped Hayley relax and relieved any pain in her elderly joints. The best thing about hydrotherapy was that she didn't ever see it as another 'treatment', it was just a fun day out with her daddy splashing around in water, yet she would be getting much-needed exercise to stop her arthritic joints from deteriorating. Hayley was a real water baby, she loved the bath and would have been happy to have daily hydrotherapy if she could.

At home Hayley behaved perfectly normally, she had the innocence of a toddler and was totally unaware that she was different to the majority of kids. Hayley loved skipping along the seafront and throwing pebbles into the sea. It was odd to think that although she was young, Hayley was already facing the same health issues as many of the elderly folk who nodded politely as we passed them on the prom.

Whenever we took her out in her pushchair, Hayley's big blue smiling eyes and frail features always attracted the attention of strangers who would just stare awkwardly. To counteract this I taught her a trick to deflect the unwanted attention of anyone who stared at her for too long. I wouldn't have minded if these people had spoken to us, asked me why she looked different, I could have educated them with the little knowledge I had about progeria. But to stare was just plain rude.

'Can I do it now, Mum?' Hayley would whisper to me.

'Go on then,' I would reply and she would stick out her tongue causing the 'starer' to quickly look away and move on. It was naughty, I know, but it gave both Hayley and me a wicked sense of satisfaction to watch their embarrassment.

Two months after her diagnosis, Hayley turned two. She

had grown very little and was still wearing clothes made to fit a three- to six-month-old baby but Mark and I wanted to make it special and showered her in presents. Like every other toddler at the time she was obsessed by the Teletubbies. It was a daily ritual for her to sit glued to the television as the brightly coloured, podgy characters with TVs in their tummies ran around in Tellytubbyland and said 'Eh-oh'. For her birthday we splashed out and bought her the set of Teletubby toys. There was Tinky Winky the purple one, Dipsy was green, Po was red. But her favourite was Laa-Laa, the yellow one. She carried it around everywhere with her. They were only 10 inches high but at that point the toys were almost as big as Hayley and she would wrestle with them. To transport them around we bought her a pram, shaped like a lady bug, which she could just about manage to hold on to.

From my first conversation with Doreen there had been one thing that stuck in my mind: 'make every minute count'. There was no doubt in my or Mark's minds that Hayley was our special girl, but I wanted to make her life even more extraordinary. 'I want to take Hayley to Disney World,' I said to Mum one morning in January as we were making breakfast.

'Where are you going to find the money to do that?' she challenged. She was right. I had given up my job at the prep school to care for Hayley after she was born, Mark was earning barely more than minimum wage on his delivery van rounds. We had no savings, our old Ford Sierra needed hundreds of pounds to be spent on fixing the rust to get it through its MOT. We had not been able to afford a family holiday the summer after Hayley was born and here I was thinking of jetting off to Florida on a trip that would cost at least £5,000. That kind of money could buy us a nearly new car, one that would fly through its

MOT. What was I thinking?

'We could set up a fund, do events, raise money. We could tell the local paper and they can run a story on Hayley. I've read stories about other kids who are sent on dream holidays, why not Hayley?' I explained to Mum, who looked at me as if I had lost leave of any tiny bit of sense I had.

'But what if you can't raise the money? What will you do then? You can't disappoint Hayley, and the girls.'

'Then I'll get a bank loan.' For the first time in months I felt positive. Raising money for Hayley gave me a focus. I was on a mission.

I waited until office hours and rang the news desk at the *Bexhill-on-Sea Observer*. I told them about Hayley and her one in eight million disease and how her family and friends were raising money to send her to Disney World. They were astounded. That afternoon they sent a reporter and photographer to our house in Bexhill and interviewed Mark and me and took pictures of Hayley.

On Friday January 7 2000, Hayley's story made front page news. 'Why friends want to give little Hayley a Disney treat', the headline read. Below it was a photo of Mark and me holding Hayley between us. The story related how Hayley was one of only three children in the UK with the rare genetic condition progeria which made her age eight times faster than normal children. It explained how her life expectancy was 13 and how Mark and I had set up a trust fund and friends and family were working to raise money to take her to Disney World. The photograph said more than any words could. Hayley looked her cutest, grinning for the camera.

Very soon after Hayley's diagnosis, Mark and I agreed that we wouldn't shield her from the public gaze. Until that day when the doctor handed us the slip of paper we had never heard of progeria and neither had any of our family and friends. With so few cases in the world, it was safe to say there was a lot of public ignorance about it. Mark and I made a conscious decision to tell the world – and that meant appearing in the media.

When the local paper hit the newsstands it opened the floodgates for what has become a lifelong media circus. Hayley's progeria story was picked up by one of the UK's leading broadsheet newspapers: the *Daily Telegraph*. As soon as the story ran in the *Telegraph* the frenzy started; my phone was red hot. I had calls from news agencies, women's magazines, television companies, radio stations, all wanting exclusive access to Hayley's amazing story. I called Mark at work panicking about what I should do and, even in the few minutes I was on the phone, six journalists had left messages for me to call them back. While I was on the phone being interviewed by one magazine, there was a knock on the door. I opened it to be handed a telegram. It was from Richard and Judy, who at the time were the brightest stars in daytime TV. Their mid-morning programme was required watching for mums like me. They wanted to whisk us up to London to appear on their show that week. We said yes and within 48 hours we were sitting being interviewed live by the most famous presenters on British TV. It was more than we had hoped for and we took the opportunity to spread the word about progeria. As we sat on the sofa with Richard and Judy one viewer called in to donate a computer having heard us talk about how difficult it was to find out information about progeria. It was incredible, in those days the average home computer cost more than £1,000 and there was a complete stranger offering to give us one.

The money flooded in too. People we had never met would be calling to donate money and gifts.

As word of Hayley's condition spread through newsrooms around the world, we appeared on TV stations from Germany to Japan. We were also contacted by James Routh, a documentary film maker who wanted to make a 30-minute programme about Hayley. For almost 12 months James and his film crew followed Hayley, Mark and me as we followed our daily routines at home in Bexhill. At first Hayley was shy when James started asking her questions about progeria, but as the months went by she began to relax. Hayley had turned four when the programme was broadcast on Channel 5 in September 2002 as part of the series of *Extraordinary People* documentaries. Titled 'The Girl Who Is Older Than her Mother' it showed Hayley from her diagnosis to her first day at school. After it was first screened, the reaction to Hayley's story was amazing.

With help from his friend, Mark set about creating a website for Hayley with our new computer. Hayley's Progeria Page was a dedicated space which gave information about Hayley's condition and documented our fund-raising efforts. As technology developed it would become a gallery showing photographs of the memorable events in Hayley's life, giving news about her health, featuring links to other progeria information sites and links for online donations to Hayley's Fund.

As a family we also worked hard to boost Hayley's Fund. Any money we were paid for magazine interviews went straight into the pot. Our local paper was also a great support in helping to publicise our efforts. For our first fundraiser Mark's sister and I were photographed at the local Toni and Guy salon – where we had our heads shaved for the cause.

The biggest donation came from a group of firemen in Hastings who saw Hayley's story in the local press and rang in offering to run the Hastings Half Marathon to help raise money. Organised by the Hastings Lions Club every March, the marathon was ranked in the top five road races in Britain and attracted around 5,000 runners including some of the world's most famous Kenyan and Ethiopian runners. On the day of the race Hayley, Mark and I stood near the starting line and cheered as the fit firemen, including one dressed in a fluffy purple dinosaur costume, ran the 13.1 mile course. As the runners made their way through the old town then back along the sea front we followed them in a replica steam train, which a group of local rail enthusiasts had kindly offered as our mode of transport for the day. Once again we were touched by the kindness of strangers and the firemen later presented Hayley's fund with a cheque for £10,000 which was more than enough to cover the cost of Hayley's Disney dream trip.

The following September we flew out to Florida with Stacey and Charlotte for the holiday of a lifetime. No one in our circle of friends had ever been to America before. It was all so exotic and exciting. We packed in everything we could in those two weeks, visiting as many theme parks as we could manage. Mark and the girls rode the Jurassic Park roller coaster at the Universal studios while Hayley and I stood at the side waiting for them. With hindsight Hayley, who was just a couple of months short of her third birthday, was too young to take it all in. Even when she came face-to-face with the king of Disney World, Mickey Mouse, in a personal meet and greet, which had been pre-arranged by one of the UK women's magazines, she was slightly bemused by everything that was happening around her. Yet for us as a family, the trip was a turning point. It gave Mark and me time to talk about how we felt.

Chapter 5
Kerry
One Big Happy Family

THE MILLENNIUM YEAR TURNED out to be a globe-trotting one for little Hayley. As well as our family holiday to Florida we were also invited to Washington DC for our first ever Sunshine Progeria Reunion. Every year The Sunshine Foundation charity for terminally ill children would arrange for all the progeria children in the world to meet up for a week-long holiday. They would pay for Mark and me to attend and take Stacey and Charlotte too. Mark was thrilled at the idea of meeting other parents and advancing his thirst for knowledge. I, on the other hand, couldn't imagine anything worse than a hotel full of terminally-ill children and their depressed parents crying over their short lifespans and mourning the fact there was no cure.

As Mark went about applying for passports, converting our spending cash into dollars and organising our travel, I worked myself into such a state about the trip I made myself physically sick. I was not ready to face up to so many other children suffering the same illness as Hayley.

'We can't go all the way to Washington DC if I'm going to throw up. It will be no fun for anyone,' I tried convincing Mark that it would be a good idea to stay home. But he pressed ahead and insisted we go shopping for summer clothes. Mark had been doing his online research and discovered Washington was expecting temperatures of 90 degrees, so we stocked up on light cotton T-shirts and shorts sets for Hayley and summer dresses for Charlotte and Stacey. It was with great reluctance that I helped pack our suitcases on the night before our departure. If Mark's girls hadn't been so excited about going on their first American adventure, I would have gladly cancelled the trip and stayed at home. But I couldn't let them down.

When we arrived at the Marriott Renaissance Hotel in Washington after a 16-hour journey, it was nothing like I could ever have expected. On checking into our room, we went down to the poolside area to meet the other families. As we got closer to the pool, we could hear the laughter and splashes of dozens of children having fun. Walking through the glass doors that led out onto the pool area, I felt a lump in my throat. It was like a saucepan full of boiled eggs – dozens of bald-headed children bobbing around in the water without a care in the world, all inhibitions thrown to the warm Washington wind. It was Hayley's cue for play. 'Can I go swimming, Mum?' she asked. I took her and the girls back to our room to change into their costumes, while Mark stayed at the pool making new friends.

Hayley was only three and was too young to take in the importance of the gathering but for Mark and me, it felt like we had found our true family. There were 27 of the 40 known cases in the world in that hotel, some were playing around in the water, others were too frail to play and sat in their wheelchairs at the water's edge, smiling in the sunshine. It finally hit me how fortunate we were to see Hayley running and playing.

Over the seven days Mark and I made valuable friendships with families from America and Europe.

We met Doreen, our friend from the UK who had first told us about the reunion, in turn she introduced us to a Dutch couple called Marjet and Klaus who ran the Progeria Family Circle linking families across Europe. Their son Ben had passed away five years earlier but they devoted their time to supporting and caring for other families. We also met our American 'phone friends' Leslie and Scott, who had already been so vital in helping us to understand Hayley's condition. For the first time we got to know older progeria children. There was 13-year-old Joscha from Germany and his best friend Mihailo from Belgrade. Both boys were quick-witted and funny to be around. Then there was Sarah, a seven-year-old Swiss girl, who could have passed for Hayley's older sister. The one thing that all these children had in common, apart from their illness and the similar bird-like features, was that they brought sunshine into the lives of everyone who knew them, including Mark and myself.

At our first reunion we met up with two other families from the UK whose children also suffered from Hutchinson-Gilford Progeria. There was a young boy from Leeds whose progeria was quite advanced and was very poorly, and a five-year-old girl called Maddie, whose family also lived in England. She immediately took a shine to Hayley. Looking at them they could even have been sisters. Maddie was almost three years older than Hayley – or 24 progeria years – but they immediately struck up what would become a close and life-long friendship. Although we had spoken to Maddie's parents on the phone and we had mutual friends, we had never met as a family. We immediately bonded with our shared experience of progeria, helped along by a few tequila shots at the hotel bar.

For the children the reunion was just one never-ending

play day. Everywhere they looked there was something for them to do. Face painting, things to make, tables laid out for drawing, colouring and cutting out shapes, ball games in the pool. There was a whole community atmosphere with teams of volunteers from the neighbourhood helping to ensure that there was never a moment when the children could be bored. We were taken out on day trips to theme parks and taken out for ribs and burgers at the local steak house.

An important part of the reunion was the question and answer session with doctors and experts. While the children were being cared for by some of the volunteers, the parents had the chance to sit around and discuss new discoveries and share the wealth of their own experience. It was at these sessions we first found out about the build-up drink, Nutrini, which some of the other children were taking. We also came to understand the different types of progeria. Hutchinson-Gilford, which Hayley had been diagnosed with, was the most common and was what the Progeria Research Foundation called 'classic' progeria. There was another type of progeria called Werner's Syndrome or 'adult onset progeria', which starts after puberty and affects growth in children in their late teens and adults in their twenties. The ageing symptoms are similar but the young people with Werner's Syndrome had longer life expectancies. Bloom's Syndrome we discovered is a variation which was first thought to affect Eastern-European Jews but has since been found in other ethnic groups including Indian, Ethiopian, Latin American, French-Canadian, Japanese, and Turkish people. Their average life expectancy is 35 and they are sensitive to sunlight and prone to leukaemia.

Our first experience of the reunion had been a real

education. But when the time came to say goodbye there was added poignancy. The children were not just saying 'so long' to their new friends, there was an air of uncertainty for the parents. We did not know which children would be playing in the pool next time we met up. This hit home the following year when we flew out to Philadelphia for our second reunion and Joscha and Mihailo were missing. In the intervening twelve months both boys had passed away. They had both been thirteen when we first met them and it shocked Mark and me to realise that in ten years time it could be Hayley who would be missing from the reunion. Thankfully Hayley was too young to notice and although saddened by the news we were reminded of a poem which Marjet of the Progeria Family Circle would send to bereaved parents.

Dying only means moving into a nicer house.
We have only gone into the next room.
We still are what we have always been.
We aren't far away.
We are only on the other side of the pathway.

The following year there was one more face missing at the reunion at the Marriott Renaissance Hotel in Orlando, Florida. Mine. I had given birth to our son Louis just two days earlier and as much as I didn't want to miss out on the fun in Florida, there was no way I could drag a tiny baby across the Atlantic.

As I helped Hayley pack her tiny shorts and vests and sundresses into her miniature pink trolley suitcase I felt a pang of jealousy. 'Night, night, see you in America,' Hayley said to her doll as I helped her close the lid. That night, tucked up in bed in her Winnie the Pooh sleepsuit, Hayley hardly slept with the excitement of knowing that the next day she would meet up with her best friend Maddie and all the other children.

When the plane touched down in Orlando, Mark called to say they were safe and the heavens had opened. I could hear the rain beating down in the background as Hayley told me she was missing me. It was the only reunion where it rained all week, so it made me feel less jealous knowing I had chosen the wettest year to stay at home. Throughout the week, Mark and Hayley rang twice a day, Hayley wanted to say hello to her new brother. She was more than 4,000 miles away from home, surrounded by friends, but she still had thoughts for little Louis.

For my next update, Mark called to say that Hayley had been a media star that day. As usual the local press turned up to interview the children. Journalists were fascinated by progeria children and with 32 families, three-quarters of the known cases in the world, on their doorstep it was too good a story to miss.

'The local TV station wanted to talk to Hayley, but she went all shy on them,' Mark said.

'You would have laughed if you'd seen her, Kerry. She was sitting on my lap wrapped in a towel with this pair of enormous sunglasses on her head like she was some superstar diva. When the reporter put the microphone up to her face and asked her if she had made friends, I think she was a bit scared as she just went quiet. The microphone was as big as her, so that may have frightened her but she went all camera-shy and just nodded. I've never seen her so quiet.' When I saw the video later I could see why they chose her for their interview, I may have been biased as her mother, but she did look super cute.

The following day there was bad news from Orlando. One of the progeria children had died in his sleep at the reunion. In the few years we had been attending, Greg Mercer from Georgia, USA, had been the VIP of the events. At 32 he was the oldest known case and had lived almost three times his life expectancy. He had a different form of progeria and had been to every one of the reunions since they started 20 years ago. With his deep southern accent he charmed the parents and volunteers alike. He had seen many friends die of premature old age, and he outlived them all. He was like the wise old man of the Progeria Reunion.

'We were queuing up for breakfast this morning when one of the parents told me Greg had been rushed to hospital in the night and had died,' Mark said. 'It was a hell of a shock.'

'How was Hayley?' was my immediate reaction. Suddenly I wanted to be by her side and to protect her.

'I don't think it has really affected her. Luckily she's too young to realise what's happened, but it's hit some of the parents hard. One of the mothers said we should all go home as it wouldn't be right to stay here in such sad times. But I and some of the other parents said it would be wrong to end it all so quickly when the other children were having such a good time. The little ones, like Hayley, were too young to understand why we were going home and it would just upset them more. Greg's family told us we should all carry on as it was what Greg would have wanted. So we've decided that, out of respect to Greg, we'll honour his memory by keeping the reunion alive.'

'And how are you?' I asked Mark.

'I feel so bad for Greg's parents. But it has made me realise how precious life is and we really have to make the most of it while it lasts as you never know what's around the corner. Some of families who were close to Greg and his parents have been having a rough time. They are probably wondering if they will be next. I've been keeping my eye on the kids, when I see one of the parents going through a bad patch, I've gone looking for their children and called them into the pool for a game of football. I couldn't bear to see them watching their parents in such a state.

'I tell you one thing, Kerry, it makes me so angry to see how unfair this disease is. These kids have done nothing to deserve it, I hope to God someone can find a cure for them.'

Another year at the reunion we met a family from Belgium who had us to thank for the diagnosis of progeria in their son. Every progeria story is heart-breaking but I felt for Wim and Godlieve Vandeweert more than anyone because their son Michiel was so similar to Hayley in age and development. Michiel was a year younger than Hayley and, like Hayley, when he was a toddler his lack of growth, thin dry skin and loss of hair had been dismissed by their doctors as 'nothing to worry about'. Fearing the condition was hereditary, Wim had a vasectomy but after seeing Hayley's first documentary alarm bells rang. Looking at Hayley was like looking at their own child, they told us. The premature ageing, the hair loss, the stiff joints, were all identical. Armed with this information, they went back to their doctor and asked if it could be progeria. After numerous tests, it was confirmed. And while they were gutted for their son, it gave them more hope for growing their family. With the tiny a one in 8 million chance of it happening again, Wim had his vasectomy reversed and in 2005 they had a baby girl, Amber. Doctors told the family that, unlike Michiel, Amber was fine. Her skin was healthy, unlike Michiel's which was translucent. Her hair was thicker than her brother's and she was a healthy weight. But within weeks of her birth Amber fell ill and, despite constant reassurance from doctors, Wim and his wife asked for her to be tested with progeria. They were devastated when the results came back as positive. After more tests it was discovered that Wim's wife carried the defective gene and their chances of having another progeria child are now 1 in 2.

'I have never won the lottery but we have had progeria twice. That is bad luck,' Wim said. I was so impressed by the family's positivity in the face of such adversity that we became good friends.

Chapter 6
Kerry
Starting School

HAYLEY'S FIRST DAY AT Sidley Primary School was something I had never dared to dream of. When we were first told that Hayley's progeria was terminal, I had rather naively assumed that Hayley would not live long enough to reach school age, yet there I was on September 4 2001 ironing her tiny uniform and making sandwiches for her big day.

As I laid out her freshly pressed blue and white checked pinafore dress and waited for her to wake up, I suddenly felt a lump in my throat. I was scared for her. For the first four years of her life Mark and I had been by her side every second of every waking hour. We made her feel like the most special person in the world because she was, in our world. We had held her hand and told her what a brave girls she was being when she cried as doctors dug needles in her looking for blood. We had lifted her up to reach the handle of the back door when she wanted to go outside to play. We had shielded her from the stares of the ignorant and the inquisitive. Now we had to hand her over to the school, and although I was sure that the head and the other teachers would do their best to protect her from bullying and educate the other children, I was still nervous about handing over responsibility.

Three months before the start of term we had attended an open day where Hayley met her new teacher Mrs Haines and some of the other children who would be in her class for the new term. It had all been a big adventure as she played shop with the other children and painted pictures. I remember how at the end of the day she had run to meet Mark and me waving a paper plate covered with glue and strands of black wool and crayoned eyes and mouth. 'This is Stacey,' she announced handing her artwork to Mark. 'She's been ever so good,' Mrs Haines reassured us.

In the months that had passed between the open day and the start of new term Hayley had already aged the equivalent of two years but she hadn't grown a centimetre. Shopping for her school uniform was a challenge. How many two-year-olds need navy school cardigans? Most of the uniforms Mark and I could find started at age 4–5 and they were swimming on her. The best we could find was a white polo shirt for a four-year-old. When we tried it on her, it reached down to her knees.

'I can tuck it in, Mummy,' she said stretching out her arms as the short sleeves reached past her tiny little elbows. She looked like she was playing dress up in her big sister Stacey's clothes. Finding a dress to fit was just as difficult. Again we had to buy the smallest we could find and even though sewing was not my strong point I turned up a large hem so the skirt wouldn't drag on the floor. Buying shoes to fit was equally challenging. Up until now she had trainers and little sandals as her feet were narrower than most children's. Finding black patent leather shoes to meet the school regulations was hard work.

'You look like a moon man,' Mark joked with her as she walked around the shop in boots that were way too big. When the shop assistant measured her feet, they were size

3 with a narrow e fitting. Eventually we found a pair of tiny black leather shoes with a T-bar which she declared were 'a gorgeous fit' as she stomped around the shop like a supermodel showing off her new footwear. 'Gorgeous! Gorgeous! Gorgeous!' she announced to the amusement of the shop assistant and other customers.

To prepare Hayley for school we had to explain to her why the progeria made her look different to other kids.

'When I get older and lose my progeria, will I have hair like Stacey?' she asked. I cuddled her and said, 'I hope so,' and crossed my fingers tightly as I said it. How could I tell her the truth that she will never grow old or grow hair unless doctors come up with a miracle drug?

The morning of her first day at school, Hayley was full of beans. She skipped into the kitchen in her fluffy pink dressing gown. I made her favourite breakfast: scrambled egg. Then she washed and brushed her teeth and I helped her get dressed in her new uniform. As I buttoned up her blouse, hitched up her skirt and helped her buckle her shoes, I felt so proud. For the finishing touch, I tied a navy blue bandana to match her cardigan around her head. She had lost all her hair when she was three and it had never really bothered her. But starting school with other, ordinary kids had made her more self-conscious and she refused to go outside without covering her bald head. She had started wearing pretty pink bonnets and baseball caps when we went out. But for school I had bought her a selection of her trademark bandanas.

In the kitchen her Powder Puff Girls lunch box was waiting, packed with a chocolate spread sandwich, a packet of crisps and her favourite Pink Panther wafer. I hoped it would be enough to maintain her energy levels throughout the day. With Louis in the pushchair, Mark and I walked her to school, followed by a crew of TV cameramen who were still making the Channel 5 documentary. Being so young Hayley thought it was perfectly normal to have an entourage following you around.

At the school door Mrs Haines met us and we waved goodbye. I tried hard not to cry. There were other first-time mums in the yard, nervous for their children's big day, but I had more reason to be afraid. Hayley already had the body of a 32-year-old. One little bump and she could break her arm.

At regular intervals throughout her primary school life Mark and I met with Hayley's teacher for progress reports and to share any worries. We were concerned that she might be falling behind in her school work due to the number of days off for hospital appointments. We also wanted to ensure that she wasn't getting bullied. She was such a cheerful child, I thought I would be able to spot the signs if she was being called names. Her personality and childhood innocence had protected her so far but her insistence on covering her head in public made me think another child had said something to her.

Mrs Haines told us that she was not lagging behind in her school work. 'She does have more time off than most of the other children but she works hard to catch up. And she is popular with the other children because of her sunny nature: she brings out the best in the others.'

'Has she been bullied because of her bald head?' I asked. 'Having no hair has never seemed to bother her until she started school. Now she refuses to go out without her bandana? Have any of the other children said anything to her?'

Mrs Haines told us there had been a 'conversation' with some of the other children who asked her why Hayley doesn't have hair. They wanted to know if she will ever grow hair. She then explained how the class had been given a lesson about differences, where she explained how we are all different: some of us have brown hair, some of us have blue eyes, some of us are tall, Hayley has no hair and we have no choice over these matters.

I was satisfied that the school would do everything they could to protect Hayley from cruel name-calling. And her academic progress was good. I just wished that there was something that could be done to help her progeria. It frustrated me that no matter how hard we tried to make Hayley's life better and spread the word about her condition, there was nothing we could do to further medical advances.

'There ain't no cure for old age,' Mark would say in his philosophical way. And he was right up to a point. He said that it would be a waste of money to spend millions of pounds in research for a condition that affects so few people when there are millions of people dying of cancer or AIDS every year. But that was no comfort to me. Some days when Hayley complained of joint pains we would be annoyed and ask ourselves, 'Why more can't be done to research this terrible illness?'

While Hayley was learning her ABC and numbers at school, Mark and I were learning more about the progerin protein which causes progeria. We heard about the Geno Project, where scientists were trying to find the bad gene that causes progeria. They had already made progress by cloning the progeria gene which they had in a database alongside all the other genes that make up human beings, but they hadn't yet worked out how to find it. They reckoned it was a lot like hunting a serial killer. They knew the killer was out there but they didn't know what it looked like. We lived in hope that with humans living longer and more people reaching old age, these scientists would find a cure while Hayley was still at primary school.

Chapter 7
Hayley
No Hair, no Nits

THE DAY I STARTED school I don't really remember very much about it but I had a film camera following me. Mum said they were making a programme about me for television. I thought that all children went on television when they started school, until Mum told me that it was because I had progeria. When I asked what progeria was, she said it meant that I was very special because only one in eight million children had progeria and that's why I was little and didn't have much hair. I remember thinking that if I was special I must be a princess or something.

When I first started school I didn't mind that I didn't have much hair because I knew I had progeria. One day the man with the camera who was making the programme about me asked if I minded having no hair. I said, 'It doesn't worry me.' Then I told him a funny story. I said 'One day someone said to me if you had a wish what would you wish for. I said nits. Because other people have hair they can get nits and I don't.' The man with the camera thought that was funny. When I look at the old videos of me on TV, it makes me laugh because I was so little.

One day in school I remember my teacher Mrs Haines told us about being different. She called John and

Samantha out to stand in front of the class. 'What colour eyes does John have?' she asked us.

We all said 'blue' because they were the same colour as mine.

'And what colour eyes does Samantha have?'

'Brown,' we said.

Then she asked if they could change the colour of their eyes. I thought it would be cool if you could change the colour of your eyes. I would have pink eyes because pink is my favourite colour. But Mrs Haines said we can't change the colour of our eyes. 'That's just the way we are. They were born with blue and brown eyes,' she said. Then she called Kyle out to the front of the class and asked us what colour hair he had and if he could change it. I thought that might be a trick question because you can change hair colour. When me and Mum were out shopping once we saw one of her friends and her hair was red. Mum said she had dyed her hair. I didn't know hair could die and thought maybe that's what happened to mine.

Kyle's hair was almost white, but Mrs Haines says it's called blond. 'Kyle has blond hair. That's who he is.'

Then she called me out in front of the class and asked the other kids, 'Does Hayley have hair?'

The other kids said no. 'Can she do anything to change it?' Mrs Haines asked.

'No, Miss,' they said.

'Repeat after me, we are who we are,' she said. 'We are who we are,' we said.

Even though my teacher said we can't do anything to change who we are, sometimes I still felt different having no hair. Mum bought me some hats and a bandana and now I wouldn't go out without wearing one. I don't mind going around the house with a bare head but I always wear a bandana outside. That's my trademark now. I have lots of different coloured ones but my favourite is pink. I don't like people staring at my head in school or when we go shopping. When I was little Mum told me I could stick my tongue out at people when they stared at me. I don't have to do it so much now because people don't stare so much now. They come and say, 'Hello, Hayley,' because they have seen me on television and in the newspapers. It is almost like I am famous or something.

The day I first started school I met my best friend Erin who started at the same time as me. She is exactly one month older than me. Her birthday is November 3 and mine is December 3.

I remember Erin because she was sitting in the corner on her own playing a Thomas the Tank Engine game on the computer. I noticed her because she always wore a jumper, even when it was hot. She was scratching herself all the time and the other kids called her 'spotty' and 'beetroot' because she had red skin that was always itching. I didn't care and went over and said, 'Hello, my name is Hayley. Why are you scratching?' She said she had something called severe eczema that made her skin get all red and itchy so she never took her jumper off, even in the summer.

'I have got progeria and I can't run or play It,' I said. I wanted Erin to be my friend because she was different like me, but she was bigger. When I played hide and seek in school I couldn't catch the other kids because they ran too fast, but Erin didn't run away. She has always stood by me because that's what best friends do.

Chapter 8
Kerry
Growing Up

WITH EACH PASSING YEAR the progeria began to leave its mark on Hayley. Throughout her primary school years her body took on the features of old age, she lost more and more fat and her frame grew thinner. Mark would call her a 'bag of bones'. The most obvious sign of change was the loss of her hair. While we were on holiday in Disney in 1999, her last strands of hair fell out. She only had one tuft left on the back of her head but she begged me to have it braided in a pretty pink hair wrap. When the wrap came out several weeks later, it took her final strands of hair with it. At the time this was more upsetting for me than Hayley because it was an obvious sign of her deterioration and I knew that without a miracle it wouldn't grow back. I still have it today, tucked away in a special box along with her first hospital gown and the nametag she was given when she was born. They are the bittersweet memories we keep.

Emotionally she started to grow up too. Like many other children of her age she started to develop a mind of her own and became more stubborn. If she didn't want to do anything, no amount of persuasion could get her to change her mind. This sometimes proved difficult when we had to visit the doctors and bribery would often come into play – a new toy or sweets usually did the trick.

55

Fortunately she didn't need too much persuasion when it came to our six-monthly check-ups with her cardiologist Dr Graeme Whincup at the Conquest Hospital, Hastings. Heart disease is the most common killer in progeria children so it has always been important to check for thickening of the arteries or any other signs or irregularities that could indicate her heart is growing old. At first I think she had a little bit of a crush on Dr Whincup because he was young, blond and handsome. She was fascinated by the large collection of coloured bow ties he used to wear and she was always made to feel special because he treated her like a best friend rather than just another patient. In order to check the condition of her heart Dr Whincup takes regular echocardiograms which use ultrasound waves to show the outline of Hayley's heart on a monitor. That way he can see if the valves and chambers are all in order and pumping blood around the body as they should. Another regular test is the electrocardiogram (ECG). To do this he used sticky patches to attach electrodes to Hayley's arms, legs and chest which gave a reading of her heartbeats and would show any signs of enlargement. He also monitors her blood and checks her cholesterol levels. The cardio visits have always been an anxious time for us as we never know when an abnormality will appear inside Hayley's body. It was, and still is, a relief when the tests come back as normal and we are reassured that Hayley's vital organ is not deteriorating.

Late one night, when Hayley was around six years old, I woke up in a panic. I heard Hayley cry out, 'Mummy, I've got a pain in my chest.' I rushed into her bedroom where she was sitting up in bed, looking grey. I felt her forehead; it was clammy. 'It feels like someone is sitting on my chest,' she whimpered. My immediate thought was, are we losing her? With no time to waste to call an ambulance, I bundled her into the car and shot to the nearest Accident and Emergency unit, jumping red lights en route. Eight minutes later Hayley was rushed into the cardio unit and hooked up to an ECG machine. I spent the rest of the night beside her bed, watching the monitor for any changes, willing her to be all right. When she woke up the following morning, she seemed much better, the colour was back in her cheeks and the doctors were happy that her heartbeat was back to normal. We were told she had suffered a supraventricular tachycardia or SVT for short. Doctors explained to us that it was nothing to worry about and was usually caused by intense excitement, stress or fright. We had been to a bonfire party the night before it happened and it was possible that the excitement of the fireworks had set her heart racing. We were just relieved it had not been more serious.

Around this time in her life our family was introduced to a new type of care for Hayley. Jane Streeter was a palliative care nurse who worked for our local hospice for terminally ill children, Demelza James House. When it was first suggested that she could help us, Mark and I were sceptical.

'We don't need a care worker. We know how to look after our own child and we can answer any questions she might have,' Mark said. I agreed with him up to a point. It seemed to be a slight on our ability as parents to have outside intervention. But, once we were introduced to Jane, it became apparent that she was going to be a valuable friend to us all. Jane was an experienced bereavement counsellor and play worker all rolled into one and was able to talk to Hayley about her child-like concerns in a way that Mark and I couldn't. By combining play and conversation, Jane quickly built up a trust with Hayley. She became another of Hayley's friends, who would take her out to the park or swimming pool and stay indoors and cook and colour with her. Their time together was private and special and as Hayley became more inquisitive it became obvious that Jane's intervention was essential when coping with difficult inquisitions.

Death was the big question. From the day of Hayley's diagnosis it had hung over us like a giant boulder which could drop anytime without warning, causing major damage. As parents of a progeria child thoughts of death were always in the back of our minds, especially when we attended the Progeria Reunions and learnt that several children, who had seemed perfectly healthy the previous year, had died in the previous 12 months. Initially Hayley was too young to register the terminal nature of her illness and that of children like her, but we knew that one day the subject would naturally arise and we would need to arm ourselves with an answer that wouldn't frighten her. Mark's attitude was 'there's no point in worrying about it, it will just make us older and greyer than we already are. Just take it as it happens.' But I couldn't be so blasé, I couldn't risk saying the wrong thing and causing emotional damage to our happy little girl.

'Does Hayley know her life expectancy?' Jane once asked me when we were alone. 'No, she doesn't need to know. The average age for a child with progeria is 13, but some die as young as six,' I confided in Jane. 'One girl died last year and she was 22. So it's hard to tell. At the moment she hasn't mentioned it but we know as she gets older there will be more questions. Sometimes it's hard being her parents. We want to protect her but we also want to be honest with her.'

'You need to be careful of what you need and what Hayley needs,' Jane replied. 'For a child her perception of

Six months
old, June 1998

Me at one year
old, 1998

With my half-sisters Charlotte, right, and Stacey, left, 2000

Me, Nanna and Pops, 2007

Me and Mum on the way to our first ever
Progeria Reunion in America, 2000

Me and Mum at an American steakhouse during the Progeria Reunion, 2003

Having fun painting at a Progeria Reunion, 2001

Riding my bike by the beach at Bexhill-on-Sea, 2002

Dressing up as Princess Hayley at the Progeria Reunion, 2003

My first day at Sidley Primary School, September 2001

Pretending to be an angel watching over my Mum at the
Progeria Reunion, 2003

Me and Mum, Christmas 2001

Holding my
10-day-old brother
Louis, 2002

life is very innocent. Hayley will ask awkward questions when you least expect it. You need to prepare yourself. You will be rushing to get ready for school one morning and she might ask the question you're dreading: "Mummy am I going to die?" Answer her and say, "We need to talk about it later, that's a big subject." But be honest – we are all going to die sometime. Trust me, I am used to dealing with children who have terminal illnesses and that's the best way to answer.'

Watching Hayley and Jane together gave me confidence. They had a special friendship, as well as a patient's confidentiality. Hayley knew if she passed a secret on to Jane, it was safe. And Jane was able to give us the reassurance we needed about Hayley's state of mind at a time when I was still too emotional to cope alone. 'She wants to protect you and is careful what she says in front of you because she doesn't want to upset you,' Jane explained.

As the progeria progressed we noticed changes in Hayley. Her arthritis worsened to the point where we saw she was unable to straighten her fingers or bend down to put her shoes on. Like an old person, she needed special adaptations around the house to help her lead an independent life.

Jane would sometimes take her out for the day to give Mark and me the chance to meet with an occupational therapist in order to assess Hayley's ability to do daily tasks and to recommend adaptations to make her life easier. There was a high ledge leading from the patio door down on to the garden, which was too difficult for Hayley's little legs to climb over. A step and handrail were fitted so that Mark and I no longer had to carry her out into the garden. As she started learning to wash herself and brush her teeth, we had special lever taps fitted in the bathroom so that her frail hands could turn them on. Another of the special aids she needed was a cushion for her chair at the dinner table. We had noticed she was developing a red bed-sore-type mark on the top of her thigh from sitting in one position for a long time. It was nothing for her to sit at the dinner table for an hour at a time at meal times and sores were developing. The therapist suggested a special cushion, such as they give old people, might help, but that was easier said than done. Her stubbornness turned this into another battle of wills and again I was grateful to Jane who managed to convince her it would be a good thing for her.

Her stubborn streak was not always easy to deal with and could reveal itself at the most inappropriate times. Following the broadcast of Hayley's first *Extraordinary People* documentary in the UK, a TV company from Japan came to England to spend a couple of weeks following our family around for a Japanese documentary called *Precious Life*. At the time we were happy to take part and spread the understanding of progeria across Asia. We were not aware of any Japanese cases and thought that if Hayley's programme could help one Japanese family identify the condition in their own child, just like it had with the Vandeweert family in Belgium, it would be worthwhile. Two years later the company wanted to come back and follow Hayley's progress. At the time I asked Hayley if she was happy to do another programme and she was keen on being big in Japan once again. But as the day of the Japanese crew's second visit drew nearer, Hayley started to get sulky. I couldn't work out what was upsetting her. When I tried asking her what was wrong, all I got was 'nothing'. With a little help from Jane I managed to get to the bottom of the problem. I felt like I was passing the buck once again, but I knew Jane would be able to root out the problem if there was one. Hayley admitted to Jane she was not looking forward to the Japanese TV company coming back.

'They are bossy and I get tired,' she told Jane. I was shocked and a little upset to hear this, it seemed like I was forcing her to do something that was obviously upsetting her. 'But she seemed quite keen when we asked her,' I said in my defence. Jane thought Hayley had been telling us what she thought we wanted to hear rather than what she really felt. I was devastated that something which seemed so straightforward had caused her this anguish and didn't want to make her do anything that she was not happy with. On the other hand the Japanese crew had already booked their flights and scheduled the film. With this in mind I called them and came to a compromise – filming will be less obtrusive than last time and their filming sessions will be shorter. Everyone seemed happy, the film was made and there were no more sulks from Hayley.

Chapter 9
Hayley
Doctors and Days Out

LIVING WITH PROGERIA IS hard. People treat you like you are a baby. I want to shout at them, 'I'm not a baby.' They say I can't do stuff like run around properly and Mum worries that if I run I will fall over and hurt myself. It's really annoying.

The worst thing about having progeria is all the blood tests and needles and stuff. Ever since I was little I have had to see lots of different doctors. My favourite is Dr Whincup. He is really nice. Whenever I see him he gives me a big hug. He's not like a doctor although he talks like one and says really long words. But he explains the long words to me and I like that. Because he's more of a heart doctor, he doesn't do things that hurt me like taking blood.

Dr Whincup does something called ECGs, which is when I have jelly put on my chest so that he can watch my heart on TV. Before I have the ECG I have to lie on the bed in Dr Whincup's room. He always says to me, 'I bet you can't leap up onto the bed.' And I always tell him, 'I bet I can.' I have to run and jump as high as I can because the bed is very high. But I never quite make it and Mum or Dad have to help me up. Once I'm on the bed Dr Whincup's nurse helps me undo my blouse and puts the jelly on my chest, then she puts wires on my chest. The jelly is cold and slimy. Then Dr Whincup points to my heart on the TV and so I can see it beating.

When I first saw my heart on TV it looked really weird. It wasn't like the TV at home; it was black and white and fuzzy. Dr Whincup always lets me look at the pictures. He says things like, 'Your numbers are good and your pictures are good,' which makes Mum and Dad happy. And he always winks at me. I used to think he was called Dr Whincup because he always winks. When it's time to go home Dr Whincup always kneels on the floor and shakes my hand and says, 'See you in six months.' I hold on to his hand and shake and shake and shake. I keep shaking his hand and won't let go. It's our little game. He always laughs and says, 'You can let go now.' It's fun. Sometimes I think if I didn't have progeria I would never get to meet cool people like Dr Whincup.

Whenever I had to see a doctor I would have the day off school. Some days I was allowed to stay home from school because my friend Jane was coming to see me. Jane was a grown-up but she was like a best friend, like Erin and Maddie. When she came to see me we would do lots of fun things like cooking and making things. Sometimes she would teach me how to cook. I remember one time we made a pizza for Mum and Dad's tea. She asked me what topping I wanted to put on it. I said ham and mushroom because I knew Dad liked mushrooms and Mum liked ham. Then Jane took me to the shop to buy all the things we need to make it. I got to push the trolley. 'Don't crash,' Jane said. But I did. I pushed the trolley into the shelf with tomatoes and it went bang. Then I got stuck and Jane had to help me move it back out. I found the mushrooms but I couldn't reach the scale to weigh them, so Jane had to lift me up. When we got back home Mum and Dad were in the living room talking to a woman who was writing things

64

down on paper. So Jane took me into the kitchen and we made our pizza. It was weird because quite often when Jane came to see me there would be strange people with Mum and Dad. I never knew why. When the pizza was ready Jane helped me to put it on a plate and I carried it into the living room for Dad. The writing lady had gone. Dad said it was the best pizza he ever tasted and I felt so proud.

Another time Jane took me swimming. On the way to the pool I was sitting in the back of Jane's car in my special car seat. Jane said to me, 'Is your leg hurting? Maybe you need a softer seat?' I didn't know how she knew my leg was sore because I hadn't told her. I thought that Mum must've told her because when was bathing me I cried when she was washing my legs and she noticed it was red. Mum said I had a bed sore, which I thought was odd because I was in the bath not bed.

'I don't care if my leg is sore,' I told Jane.

'But I care,' said Jane. 'I don't want you to get sores. It might stop you going swimming and doing other things that you enjoy.' I thought about it. I liked swimming. Dad would take me every week for therapy and I didn't want to stop going just because I had a sore.

'OK I'll have a cushion,' I said. Soon after that I got a new cushion to sit on when I was having my food at the table. It wasn't very comfy, but at least it stopped the sores and I didn't have to stop swimming and good stuff.

I used to tell Jane my secrets and things that I didn't like to worry Mum about. She once asked me if I had friends in school. I told her I was very popular and had loads of good friends. But I said I didn't like it if everyone is like, 'Hello Hayley.' 'It's hard work being a star,' I told her. Jane said it's OK to be sad sometimes. I said 'Everybody has to be sad sometimes.' Jane was pleased when I said that. But I wasn't sad, I was just saying it.

My favourite toy when I was younger was my Wendy house. My Nanna and Pops made it for me as a surprise. Mum and Dad took me away and when we came back there was a house at the bottom of the garden. It was just like a real house but it was made of wood. It had pink curtains on the windows, pink fluffy cushions on the chairs and a sign saying Hayley's House. Mum always used to be afraid that I would fall and hurt myself but she liked me playing in my Wendy house because she knew I was safe. I used to pretend it was my princess castle. Whenever my friend Maddie, who also had progeria, came to play with me we would go in my castle and pretend to be princesses. I would be Princess Hayley and she would be Princess Maddie. Now I am older I don't play in my house any more because it's for babies.

Chapter 10
Kerry
Grandparents Equals Spoilt Rotten

THERE IS ALWAYS A special bond between grandparents and their first grandchild, but when that child has a terminal illness the connection is stronger. From the moment Hayley entered the world my mum was beside me in the delivery room with her camera, taking photos of little Hayley from all angles. I remember one of the nurses turned to her and said, 'You would think she was a princess.' To which my mum replied, 'She is a princess to me.' And that has pretty much summed up Hayley's place in her affections from day one.

Throughout my first months as a new mum, Mum was by my side giving me her support and first-hand advice. And when I was at my most suicidal after the progeria diagnosis, it was Mum who watched over me and gave me the verbal shake I needed when she told me, 'Don't be selfish, think of Hayley.'

Hayley was not just her granddaughter, she was almost like her fourth child. For the first years of her life I had spent many weekends with Mum and Dad. Technically speaking Derek was my stepdad as Mum had married him when I was four and my sister Janie was three. But we had never had any contact with our biological father and Derek immediately became the father figure that was missing in our family. When Mark and I were having trouble with our relationship, I would run home. And even when things were good between us Hayley still spent every weekend at her grandparents.

Nanna and Pops were the most important people in Hayley's young life – and she was the centre of their world.

It became our weekly ritual. On a Friday afternoon Hayley would wait for Pops' van to pull up so that her weekend adventure could start. Dad works as a building foreman and as soon as she saw his flatbed truck driving down around the corner she would grab her bag and stand at the door waiting. A weekend at Nanna and Pops' house usually consisted of baking cakes with Nanna or gardening with Pops. Mum worked as a school cook and was an excellent baker, so at the end of the weekend Hayley would come home with flapjacks, cookies, gingerbread men or chocolate cakes. Other times she would go shopping for clothes, knowing Nanna would indulge her and buy her anything she wanted. I remember on one occasion Hayley was so excited when Nanna bought her a bright pink strapless dress with a tutu-style skirt.

'It's hideous. I tried to persuade her not to buy it,' Mum apologised to me. 'I told her it was too big, but she said I'll grow into it. It's so big, she looks like a meringue on a lollipop stick.' Even against her better judgement, Nanna could never say no to Hayley.

In the garden Hayley would help Pops to plant bulbs or feed the koi carp in the fish pond. Like her grandparents, Hayley loved all flowers – as long as they were pink. But they never grew quickly enough for her and she would always check for growth on a daily basis, only to be disappointed.

Nanna was like a second mum to Hayley. She was just

as protective as me and equally sensitive to the comments and stares of strangers. Whenever they took Hayley out on day trips to the beach near their home strangers would stop and say, 'Isn't she lovely.' Mum would always agree with grandparental pride. But by the time Hayley reached the age of four and the baldness and thin, frail features of progeria became more obvious, Nanna became more sensitive. 'It makes me so angry, when people stare at her,' she would say to me. 'It happens all the time and I want to shout at them.' On one occasion a middle-aged couple stopped them as they were walking along the seafront at Dymchurch, and said, 'I hope you don't mind us asking, what is wrong with your little girl?' Mum explained all about progeria and how Hayley was ageing before her eyes. It was an education for both sides. Mum accepted that Hayley did look different and she could never stop people looking and the couple, who were brave enough to ask, had a better understanding of Hayley's condition. In public Mum managed to put on a brave face, but in their private moments, she worried about Hayley's future. This was particularly difficult when it came to bath time. Hayley was a real water baby and loved having a bath every night before bedtime. She would stay in as long as she could, asking for more warm water when it started to cool. For seven years Mum had worked at a care home bathing frail and elderly people every day so she was used to seeing the paper-thin, easily-bruised skin and over-sized arthritic joints on 90-year-olds. But it was hard to accept on her young granddaughter.

As soon as she was old enough Nanna and Pops converted their spare bedroom, which had been my old bedroom, into Hayley's room. They painted all the walls pink, hung pink curtains at the windows and a Piglet duvet cover on the bed. All her toys were stacked neatly on shelves and in baskets. Yet she never slept there. She would always insist on sleeping between them in their bed. Eventually they had to give in and put a mattress on the floor next to their bed at night. These bedtime intrusions turned out to be quite useful, while snuggling together in bed watching TV, Hayley would often let Nanna in on her secrets.

On one occasion, shortly after she had started school, I was getting worried that she was not eating her packed lunch. Her lunchbox was always empty when she came home, but her weight was still low and I was concerned that she was not getting the nutrition she needed. When she was at home I could see what exactly she was leaving on her plate, but in school it was difficult to monitor. One night while they were tucked up in bed, Nanna dropped the subject of school and food into their bedtime chat. 'Are you eating your packed lunch?' she asked, slyly. Hayley whispered back, 'Sometimes I give it away, but you mustn't tell Mummy, she thinks I eat it all.' With this information I was able to speak to Hayley's teachers and get them to be extra vigilant at lunch times.

Nanna also came to the rescue on the rare occasion when bullying threatened to become an issue. 'Some girls in school keep calling me names, Nanna,' she confessed.

'Take no notice of them they are just jealous,' Nanna replied.

'What do you mean jealous?'

'Well, you have so many friends and you are so pretty that they are jealous they are not like you.' With this idea in her head, Hayley was happy and bullying never really became an issue in her life.

When the all-important question of death reared its head, it was Nanna who saved the day. 'She's asking me what happens when I die. What do I tell her?' I said to Mum when we were alone. With hindsight it was the typical inquisitive question that five-year-olds have. Both Ruby and Louis would later reach the same stage in their development, when the question of life and what next is important. But with Hayley it was a more sensitive subject.

'You have to tell her the truth,' said Mum, who has always been a firm believer in honesty being the best policy.

'I don't know if I can,' I admitted. Although she understood more about her illness and why she was different, I could not trust myself to talk about death without crying and giving my true feelings away.

'Then I'll do it for you,' said Mum.

The following weekend Mum broached the subject while they were lying in bed. 'Mummy tells me you want to know what happens when you die,' she ventured. Hayley nodded. 'Well when you die you go to a better place. Some people are put in a grave in a grave yard and some people are burnt.'

'What's a gravy yard?' Hayley asked, getting her words mixed up. 'It's a place where people go after they die, before they go to heaven. When we go to the shops we drive past a grave yard. Would you like to go there?'

Hayley nodded her head. I don't think she really registered the whole concept of death and burial, it just seemed like another day out. Nanna and Pops decided it would be best to treat it just like any other day trip to the park or a museum. Together they walked around the moss-covered gravestones, reading the names and looking at the ages of the people buried below.

'This one looks like a Mummy's chest,' said Hayley walking zombie-like across one large tomb, imitating one of the characters she had seen on the cartoon Scooby Doo.

On another headstone my mum pointed out the age of a girl who had died when she was only 14 and was buried with her parents.

They talked about the difference between burial and cremation. Nanna explained that when you were cremated you were burnt.

'When I die I would like to be buried with Mummy and Daddy,' Hayley said. To her it seemed like no big deal, but Mum had to turn her head to hide her tears. To think that she could be in a grave before her Nanna was too difficult to contemplate.

Chapter 11
Hayley
The Greatest Pops in the World

MY POPS IS THE nicest granddad in the whole world. He lets me ride in his van and my Nanna is the best cook in the world.

When I was little I used to be really close to my Nanna and Pops. I would say to Mummy, 'Can I sleep at Nanna and Pops' house tonight?' If it was a Friday she would say yes.

I had my own room at their house. It was all pink, but I never slept there. I would say, 'Can I sleep with you Nanna?' and she would always let me get in bed between her and Pops. I used to sleep in between them in their bed, I was never afraid they would roll over and squash me in the night.

At night Pops used to read me a story called Chicken Licken before I went to sleep. I liked Chicken Licken, because that's Mum and Dad's nickname for me – Chicken. They said when I was a baby I looked like a plucked chicken because my legs were so skinny. In the story of Chicken Licken, he says the 'sky is falling'. When Pops read that bit to me he would say it in a funny voice and made me laugh. I liked it so much I made him read it again. Sometimes he would read it five times before I fell asleep. I knew the story of Chicken Licken wasn't true because I knew the sky couldn't fall in. The sky is where heaven is. I knew this because Nanna took me to a grave yard with a church and showed me where people are buried. It was the place where people go when they die but I thought it was called a gravy yard like the gravy you have on dinner. I was quite little when we went to the grave yard and I remember saying that when people are in their graves they don't do a single thing except sleep. I thought they couldn't have dinner, breakfast or lunch. They were fast asleep because they were dead. Nanna told me that when people die they go in a grave, and then they go to heaven. When I die I am going to go in a grave with Mum and Dad. Nanna said she is going with Pops.

I liked going to Nanna and Pops' house because they live near a park and Pops took me on the swings and watched me on the slide to make sure I didn't fall. On the way to the park we would stop at the farm shop and buy sweets. At Christmas time we went shopping and Nanna bought me stuff. One time she bought me a pink dress. It was gorgeous. I looked like a real princess but Nanna said it was too big. I said I would grow into it because I hoped that one day I would lose my progeria and grow.

I always used to get sad when I knew Mum was coming to pick me up from Nanna and Pops' house and take me home. I would cry, 'Please can I stay here, Nanna?' I never wanted to go home because I loved being with Nanna and Pops. They never shouted at each other like Mum and Dad. I felt scared when Mum and Dad were shouting, even though it wasn't at me I thought I had done something wrong. Nanna would tell me to count the sleeps and when I get to five it will be time to go back to their house.

When I got older I stopped going to Nanna and Pops' house every weekend. When I asked my mum why, she said it was because it wasn't fair on my cousins. I have five other cousins, plus Ruby and Louis and Nanna doesn't have enough beds for us all to stay. I was sad, but I know that even if I don't sleep over there all the time, they are still special to me.

I remember once when I was at the Pride of Britain Awards in London and someone famous, I think it was Prince Charles, said to me, 'Who is your favourite person?' I said, 'Pops,' and Prince Charles laughed. When I told Pops he said that was a lovely thing to say. But I was only saying the truth.

Chapter 12
Kerry
Hospices are for Living, not Dying

THE DEMELZA JAMES HOUSE in Kent was our local hospice for sick and terminally ill children. When Hayley was still at primary school her palliative nurse Jane, who was based at the centre, suggested we might like to visit with Hayley. I had heard of Demelza James House because it had a charity shop in a nearby town.

'Jane has suggested we could take Hayley to Demelza House,' I said to Mark one afternoon.

I thought it would be a nice thing to do as a family, but I wasn't prepared for Mark's reaction.

'Hospices are places where you go to die. I'm not ready for it. Hayley isn't ready for it,' Mark snapped.

'But I thought it would be a lovely retreat that we could visit as a family. It's a chance to get away from it all and relax. They have a Jacuzzi room, which will be good for Hayley's arthritis. There's a soft play area where she can run about without any worry that she'll fall and hurt herself and they have nurses and carers who watch the children and give parents a break. It's a really special place.'

I had underestimated the message I was giving out. I thought Mark would be as excited as I was for us and Hayley, but he was totally against it.

'You can go if you want, but don't expect me to come.'

That was his final answer. But I wasn't prepared to give in so easily. The atmosphere in the house was tense for a couple of days as I went ahead and planned our first visit to Demelza House. As far as I was concerned the hospice was as much about living as dying. It was somewhere we could go as a family and spend some quality time together, so I booked a family room for the weekend for me, Mark, Hayley and Louis, who was less than a year old at the time.

Explaining our weekend away to Hayley was going to need a delicate and tactful approach, so as usual in those circumstances, I passed the buck to Jane. I wasn't ready for her to know the true reason for hospices, so she told her that we would be going to a place where children go when they are not well and poorly. She also prepared Hayley for the fact that there might be some children there in wheelchairs and children who could not talk. This didn't seem to bother her and she was equally as excited about our mini holiday.

As the date of our first visit approached, Mark could see I wasn't going to back down and reluctantly came round to the idea. On the hour-long journey to Sittingbourne it felt like we were going on holidays. We had packed a suitcase with our pyjamas and swimming costumes and played I-Spy in the car on the way there. Driving up to the hospice was like entering an upmarket country house hotel. A long drive through six acres of Kent countryside brought us to a beautiful red-roofed old brick oast house.

Jane was there to greet us and showed us to our suite of rooms. It was like something from a film set. There was a big double bedroom for Mark and me, a cot for Louis and a single room for Hayley, a fully equipped kitchen where we could cook our own meals and a sitting room with a flat-screen TV. She introduced Hayley to one of the care workers who took her to the play room. Hayley was more than happy to go off and play with her 'new friend' and while she was occupied Mark and I were given a guided tour of the facilities.

'It's very luxurious,' I said to Jane as she showed us into the Jacuzzi room, which would not have been out of place in a five-star hotel.

'Yes, but most parents tell us the real luxury is having a night of undisturbed sleep,' Jane replied.

When we got to the soft play room, we saw Hayley climbing up a flight of giant red foam steps while her carer stood by. She saw us and waved, not the slightest bit bothered that we were not staying with her. In the music therapy room another of the carers was playing the piano while a severely handicapped young boy in a wheelchair was using his limited movement in his right hand to bang a drum loudly.

'That's Jamie, he has cerebral palsy. He looks forward to coming here once a month to see his friends,' Jane explained.

When he saw the other families, Mark's worst fears were dispelled. It wasn't a hospital full of dying children, it was a play centre full of children who still loved life and everything it had to offer. Meeting other children made us realise how lucky we were to have Hayley in her relatively 'normal' condition. Some children had leukaemia and only a few months to live, others who suffered from the terminal muscle-wasting disease muscular dystrophy were being pushed around in wheelchairs by their carers. These families were in a far worse situation than us and talking to other parents gave us strength. The one thing all these children had was life and hope. Yes it was noisy, but the rooms were filled with the sounds of fun. Mark later confessed that he had been pleasantly surprised. He said,

'Everyone was having such a good time, laughing and playing, I forgot where we were.'

However my parents were not so easy to convince. One afternoon after our first trip to Demelza House I had taken Hayley on a day trip to Leeds Castle with Nanna and Pops. Hayley loved feeding the swans on the castle moat. This particular afternoon, Pops had taken Hayley down to the water's edge with their bag of stale crusts, while Mum and I sat on a bench and watched them. Demelza House was the 'elephant in the room' and I tried to think of ways to bring it up without spoiling the afternoon for everyone.

'It's not how you imagine a hospice to be,' I said testing the water.

Silence.

When I first told her of my plans to visit the hospice, like Mark, she had been totally against the idea. So I tried again.

'Hayley loved it there. She said she liked the Jacuzzi best of all. But she can't say Jacuzzi so she calls it a kajuzzi.

'I don't think it's necessary to go there,' Mum retaliated. 'If I want to spend time with Hayley, Pops and I can bring her here for the afternoon; we can have her to sleep over at our house. We don't need to go there.'

Then her words stopped as she choked back her tears and looked across the lawn to Hayley who was holding her Pops' hand and looking up at him with such love as if he was the most important person in her world.

'We will go if that's what Hayley wants, but we will not go voluntarily,' were Mum's final words.

Subject closed.

The rest of the afternoon passed with no bad feeling. Our words were over but I couldn't help feeling the hospice issue was driving a wedge between our family. We took Hayley around the castle and showed her paintings of princesses from years gone by. Pops lifted Hayley up to stand in one of the old stone windows to look out over the grounds and challenged her to imagine what life would be like if she lived in a castle.

'If this was my castle, I would wait for a prince to come along and marry me,' she said.

'What will you wear on your wedding day?' Nanna asked.

'I will have a big pink dress and a tiara. Every single thing will be pink and I will be called Princess Hayley.'

Later that evening while Mum and I were cooking supper, Hayley came into the kitchen and asked 'Did you know we went to Demelza House, Nanna?'

'Yes, a little bird told me,' said Nanna, scooping Hayley up in her arms and sitting her down next to the draining board so she could watch us as we carried on making chips for supper.

'The kajuzzi was really warm and nice. Next time we go you and Pops can come too. You can wear your bathers in the kajuzzi like me.'

The subject was back up for discussion. After supper when Pops had taken Hayley to bed and Mum and I were alone washing dishes, I explained how relaxing it had been.

'When you walk through the doors you don't think of death. The atmosphere is lovely. It feels like you're really having a break.

'The only time I got upset was when they offered to take us to see the cold room. It's a refrigerated room with a bed where they can go to die, but that's in a separate wing to the rest of the rooms and you don't need to go there. I wasn't ready to see it. If you choose for your child to die there, that's the place where you go. But I'm not going to let her die there.'

'Let's not go into that this minute,' said Mum, turning her head away from me to hide her tears. She made it clear that she would not go and I didn't force the subject. Mark and I continued to visit at regular intervals. Sometimes I would take Hayley on my own, other times we would go as a family. During this time I was studying holistic therapy at college and the weekends at Demelza House gave me time to study in peace and quiet while Hayley played with her new friends. True to her word, my mum never joined us but it was never an issue any more.

Chapter 13
Hayley
Hospices are not Like Hospitals

ONE DAY MUM TOLD me we were going away to a place called Demelza House for a holiday. I like holidays. When we go to the progeria reunions it's like a holiday because we get to stay in a hotel with a swimming pool and we can play in the pool all day if we want.

My friend Jane said Demelza House was a place where children go when they are poorly. She said it was like a hospital, but a lot more fun.

'You will see people who are handicapped and make a lot of noise,' she said. I thought I had seen handicapped children before. When we went to the Progeria Reunions there was a boy in a wheelchair, who couldn't run around like me and my other friends.

When Jane said it was like a hospital, I wasn't sure that I wanted to go. It didn't sound like much fun. I like going to see Dr Whincup at hospital, but the rest of the time hospitals are just a bunch of needles and tests and I don't like them very much. I know I have to do it because of my progeria but I wish I didn't.

'Will it be like the reunions?' I asked.

'A little bit, but we are not going on a plane, we'll be going in our car,' Mum said. 'They have a big play room where you can run around, and a Jacuzzi.'

'What's a kajuzzi?' I said.

'You know. The warm pools with bubbles. You've been in one when you go to hydrotherapy,' Mum said.

'I like kajuzzis,' I said. I never knew what a hospice was but it sounded more fun than a hospital.

The first time we went was really fun. There was a big soft room and arts and crafts room. I liked the soft play room. I could jump around lots more without hurting myself. I liked painting and colouring too, but I wasn't very good at it.

There were a few other children at the hospice. At the beginning I wasn't used to seeing children in wheelchairs. Some of the children in wheelchairs were shouting and making loud noises and I was frightened. I thought, why are they shouting? but Jane told me they had learning disabilities and couldn't help it. As I got older I understood they had learning disabilities and felt really glad that I wasn't in a wheelchair.

Chapter 14
Kerry
Hayley Okines, Friend of the Stars

IN MANY WAYS HAYLEY is just like many other girls of her age – she loves playing with make-up and dancing around her bedroom to her favourite pop song of the moment. But unlike other teenage girls Hayley's progeria has paved the way for her to meet many of the stars she has plastered over her bedroom wall.

Her life in the media spotlight had brought many extraordinary twists to our lives. I remember having one of the first of many 'pinch-me, I'm dreaming' moments when we discovered Hayley had been nominated for an award at the *Woman's Own* Children of Courage Awards in 2002. The awards were being held at Westminster Abbey in London on Wednesday, December 11. HRH Prince Charles would be presenting 10 children with medals for their bravery. Hayley was being honoured for her outstanding courage having been nominated by readers of *Woman's Own* magazine, who had followed her life through magazine features.

I dressed Hayley in her best lilac satin dress, with matching purple ankle socks, pale lilac cardigan and black shoes. In her own words she looked 'gorgeous'. Before the awards the families of all the children were taken to meet the Prime Minister Tony Blair at 10 Downing Street.

Hayley struck up a friendship with the Prime Minister's son Leo, who was only two, but already the same size as Hayley. They spent the entire time sitting together on a window sill singing nursery rhymes, oblivious to the excitement that was going on around them.

On the coach from Downing Street to Westminster Abbey, the children and their parents were given a reminder of what to expect. 'There will be lots of celebrities there, so get your autograph books ready,' the host said over the coach speaker system. 'And when you meet Prince Charles remember to say please and thank you. But don't ask him for his autograph because he doesn't give autographs,' he warned

Walking into the Abbey, we felt like royalty. We couldn't believe our eyes. Everywhere we looked there was someone we recognised from TV. Burly *EastEnders* actor Ross Kemp swept Hayley off her feet and gave her a bear hug, pop star Billie Piper gave her a kiss and veteran comedian Sir Norman Wisdom tickled her bald head. When actress Suranne Jones laid eyes on Hayley's cheery face, she was so overcome with emotion she started to cry. As we sat through the ceremony we heard many poignant and emotional stories of brave and unselfish children. One sixteen-year-old boy was picking up an award for his younger brother who had been killed by a falling tree while pushing him to safety. There was a twelve-year-old girl who had saved a drowning toddler, an eleven-year-old girl who saved her sister's life when she was impaled on a metal spike and a seven-year-old girl who had been born with hydrocephalus and spina bifida and had undergone eight major operations At five, Hayley was the youngest of the children and also the smallest, so she seemed to get more than her fair share of attention.

When the time came to hand out the awards Prince

Charles knelt down to hang the red-ribboned medal around Hayley's neck. And at that point she broke the cardinal rule and asked, 'Can I have your autograph, please?' Her cheeky smile won over the royal guest who replied, 'Only if I can have yours.' Hayley scribbled her name on a piece of paper and gave it to the future king of England and he returned the favour. Hayley's audacity earned her a spot on the national *News at Ten* that night.

After the awards we made friends with some of the celebrities who volunteered to help us to raise money for Hayley's Progeria Fund. When he was appearing in theatre in neighbouring Brighton, Ross Kemp volunteered to come down to Bexhill to launch a balloon race to raise funds for Hayley's fund. As a winner of an award Hayley was also invited back to subsequent awards ceremonies where she got to meet even more stars. On one occasion she met Kimberley and Nicola from the band Girls Aloud, who invited her backstage at one of their concerts. When she got to the concert, a woman with a broad Geordie accent said to Hayley, 'Haven't I seen you on TV?' We turned around and it was Cheryl Cole. I was gobsmacked to think that a star as big as Cheryl had recognised her.

When she was six Hayley became obsessed by pop star Kylie Minogue. She would play her dance hit Spinning Around non-stop. Whenever Kylie was on TV, Mark and I would watch and laugh as Hayley wiggled her bony bum and waved her hands in time with the star. The Locomotion was another of her favourites. Her sister Stacey had taught her the moves and she would make us all join in the dance routine with her, standing together in the lounge, swinging our hips and jumping around like idiots. When Hayley was entered for the Child of Courage Award she had to nominate her greatest wish. It was an easy choice. 'I want to meet Kylie Minogue,' she said. Months had passed since the awards and I hadn't given it a second thought. Then out of the blue I got a call from Kylie's manager, saying Kylie had heard about Hayley's wish to meet her and wanted to make it come true. When we picked Hayley up from school that afternoon Mark and I asked her.

'What would be your dream come true?'

'To meet Kylie.'

'Well, she wants to meet you too.'

Hayley's face lit up as if we had given her the most precious thing in the world.

On the day of the meeting, Mark and I took Hayley, Charlotte, Stacey and Louis, to a studio in London where Kylie and all her band and dancers were rehearsing for her tour. Hayley's eyes popped out of her head when she saw some of the male dancers dressed in high-heeled boots and red masks. Then Kylie appeared and Hayley ran to her. The petite star picked Hayley up and carried her around the studio, introducing her to her band and dancers before inviting us to stay and watch the rehearsal. We sat and watched the whole run-through of her Showgirl Tour, with Kylie just inches away from us and Hayley standing beside us mimicking Kylie's every dance move. It was so cute. When it was time to leave Kylie gave us front-row tickets for her show in London the following month.

Another of those pinch-me moments came on September 29 2004 when Hayley was chosen to be the match mascot for Mark's favourite football team: Chelsea FC. In all honesty, I think Mark was more excited than Hayley to start with. He had followed the team since he was twelve in the days when Peter Osgood was captain. And throughout his life he had continued to support them, with his oldest daughter Charlotte following in his footsteps. James the documentary film maker, who was shadowing our family making the second documentary *The Girl Who Is Older Than Her Grandmother*, knew Mark's passion and arranged for Hayley to be team mascot for one of their most important matches of the season, their Champion's League match against FC Porto.

At first Hayley didn't seem that bothered, she was more excited to be having an extra day off school. Until a long black stretch limo pulled up outside our front door to take us to Stamford Bridge, then she went wild. In the limo journey to London, Hayley and Charlotte argued over who was the more excited. Whereas it was Mark who was the one who couldn't contain his excitement. As the limousine pulled up outside Chelsea's stadium, we were mobbed by fans with cameras who thought the tinted windows were hiding a football star from the public gaze. They were shocked when Hayley stepped out in her little pink hoodie and jeans and smiled for their cameras.

At the stadium we were taken to the hospitality suite and introduced to our host for the night, captain John Terry. One by one he took us to meet his team mates Frank Lampard, Joe Cole, Paulo Ferreira, Glen Johnson, Eidur Gudjohnsen, Wayne Bridge, Scott Parker, Arjen Robben and even Mark's own childhood hero Peter Osgood. Suddenly an Australian voice shouted, 'What are you doing here?' Turning around Hayley was surprised to be greeted by her pop idol Kylie. 'What are you doing here?' Hayley replied as she ran to her like a long-lost sister. They chatted like old friends, then we were whisked away to prepare for the match. We were taken to the dressing room where Hayley was given her own tiny Chelsea strip to change into before walking down to the tunnel ready for her starring moment.

'I'm so nervous, I've got butterflies in my tummy,

Mummy,' she whispered as in the distance the roar of 39,000 Chelsea fans erupted around the stadium.

Holding on to John Terry's hand, Hayley bravely walked out towards the centre of the floodlit pitch in her Chelsea kit with her pink hoodie over her shoulders to keep her warm.

'A big thank you to our match mascot, Hayley Okines!' the announcer said. Hayley beamed and Mark picked her up on his shoulders and walked across the pitch for a final lap of honour under the bright lights of Stamford Bridge. Afterwards as we walked back into the tunnel, Mark turned to me and whispered, 'I'm privileged that Hayley has given us the opportunity to do things we wouldn't normally do.'

In November 2004, Hayley had another of her wishes granted when she met the crocodile hunter Steve Irwin. She was obsessed with him and his wide-eyed adventures with the world's most dangerous animals. She would pull her little chair up in front of the TV and sit glued to the screen as he crept up on sleeping crocodiles. When dangerous snakes wound themselves around his body, she would shout 'crikey' at the TV, imitating her animal-loving hero's feigned surprise. I remember the time she met Kylie Minogue she said, 'You live in Australia, don't you? Do you know where Steve Irwin and his alligators live?' So obsessed was she with him. She finally realised her dream with the help of TV show *This Morning* who had heard about Hayley's wish and wanted to make it come true. Initially there was talk that they would fly our family out to his zoo in Queensland, which would have been an amazing experience, but Mark and I were worried that the 24-hour flight would be too difficult for Hayley. When the actual meeting took place it was much closer to home – just an hour's drive away at Port Lympne Wild Animal Park at

Team mascot for Chelsea Football Club, 2004

Dad's dream fulfilled at Chelsea Football Club

Me and TV star Ross Kemp at the
Children of Courage Awards in London, 2003

Me and TV presenter Lorraine Kelly at the
Children of Courage Awards in London, 2003

My new best friend Kylie Minogue, 2004

Me and Nicola Roberts of Girls Aloud, 2008

Backstage with Kimberley Walsh of Girls Aloud at their concert, 2008

Presenting Simon Cowell with my
Voices for Tomorrow CD, 2006

Asking Prince Charles for an autograph when I won the
Children of Courage Awards in 2002

Meeting my hero the Crocodile Hunter Steve Irwin, 2004

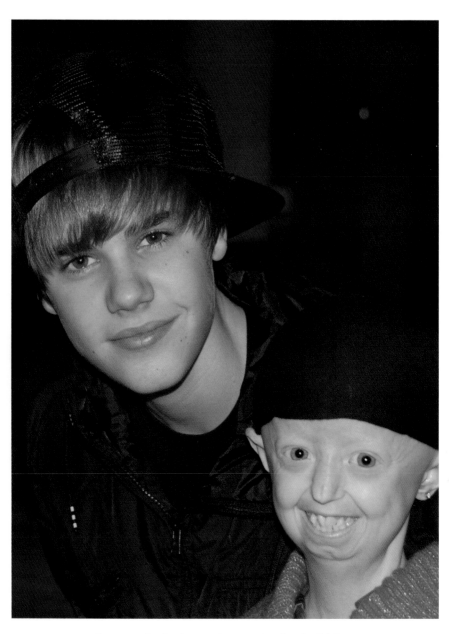

I was so lucky to meet superstar Justin Bieber
for my 13th birthday, December 2010

Port Lympne in Kent. Run by the John Aspinall Foundation, the zoo was well-known throughout the world for its conservation programmes in breeding gorillas and the almost extinct black rhinos. Crocodile hunter Steve was visiting the zoo to see their animal conservation programme in action and it was arranged that he would take time out to meet Hayley. The organisation surrounding their meeting was very cloak and dagger, we had to keep it a surprise with hushed telephone calls when Hayley was not listening.

On the morning of the meeting we woke up and there was layer of frost on the ground outside. We had told Hayley she was having a day off school to visit the zoo.

'Do we have to go today, it's too cold,' she moaned as I wrapped her up in her thickest padded pink jacket and woolly ski hat covering her ears. It was not the ideal day for a trip to the zoo, but Steve Irwin had travelled halfway around the world so we couldn't miss the opportunity.

'It will be fun. We can see the rhinos and the gorillas,' I convinced her. On arrival at the zoo we met with the head keeper and Alison Hammond, one of the reporters from the TV show *This Morning*, and were shown around the animal enclosures. Suddenly a jeep pulled up and the blond bundle of khaki-clad energy that was Steve Irwin jumped out. Hayley's face was a picture.

'Crikey!' she said in surprise.

'Crikey!' he replied in his thick Aussie accent, just like on the telly. And they both laughed. Steve was her new best friend and Hayley followed him as he introduced her to the black rhinos and fed them chocolate, which Steve told her was their favourite food. It was one of those precious moments that she has never forgotten.

Before he left Steve knelt down beside her, handed her an envelope and said, 'I know you'd like to swim with dolphins.' Inside the envelope were tickets to a marine centre in the south of France where she could live her dream. She was overwhelmed. Then with a 'See you later, Alligator' he jumped back in his jeep.

'In a while, crocodile,' Hayley replied as she waved goodbye.

Two years later we were all saddened to hear the news that this great animal lover had been killed by one of the most gentle animals, a stingray.

At one of the many awards ceremonies we were invited to attend, Hayley got to prove she had the X Factor by meeting TV and music mogul Simon Cowell. She had become a recording star in her own right when singer/songwriter Jane Winiberg saw one of Hayley's documentaries and was moved to write a song to raise money for the Progeria Research Foundation. She invited Hayley to join the Kids Choir 2000 in a studio in Southend where *Voices of Tomorrow* was recorded. Thousands of copies were made and sold in supermarkets, online and local record shops and we came close to making it into the top 40. So Hayley took the opportunity of giving Simon Cowell a copy of her CD and asking him to sign it. It may not have been up to Leona Lewis's standards, but I like to think he appreciated the effort that went into making it.

With every new star she met, Hayley felt that bit more special and the publicity that surrounded many of her celebrity encounters reinforced the message that she was special. Instead of attracting stares or hurtful comments like, 'There's that little girl who looks like a witch,' people would come up to us and say, 'Hello, Hayley.'

Chapter 15
Hayley
Being Famous Can Be Annoying

THE BEST THING ABOUT having progeria is that I get to go to really cool places and meet cool people.

When I was little Mum and Dad took me to London to the Children of Courage Awards and I met loads of famous people but I was so small I didn't know who they were.

Mum keeps loads of photos and stuff in her memory boxes. They are like shoe boxes full of things that make her remember happy times. It's fun to sit down with Mum and look through them. There are cards and letters I have written and some of my old clothes from when I was a tiny baby. And there are lots of photos of me when I was really small with lots of different people. Mum tells me they are very famous. There is a photo of me with Prince Charles. Mum told me that I asked him for his autograph when I wasn't supposed to. I was only five and didn't remember doing it but it made me laugh when Mum told me. I was so little I didn't even know who Prince Charles was. I do now. He talks posh and is a real prince. And one day he will be king.

Another time I met Kylie Minogue but it was so long ago I can't remember much about it. We went up to London to see her because Mum said I used to like dancing to her songs like Locomotion. She was dancing with loads of men and women in funny clothes. When I saw her I ran towards her and shouted, 'Kylie,' and hugged her. She let us stay and watch her dance and I was dancing as well. When she was dancing she waved at me and that made me feel special. I saw her again when I was a mascot for Chelsea. We spoke for a while. It was nice that she remembered me and wanted to see me.

The best famous person I met when I was little was Crocodile Man Steve Irwin. I used to be really interested in crocodiles and snakes. It was cool to meet him at the zoo. When I heard he had died I was really upset. I thought it was strange that he was used to handling dangerous crocodiles and he was killed by a sting ray. It made me feel really lucky I had met him when I did.

Sometimes I feel like I am famous because people I don't know come up to me and say, 'Aren't you the girl off the telly?' It's quite sweet but it can be annoying when I am with my friends. I want to say, 'Go away and leave me alone.' But I don't. That would be rude. So I just smile and say, 'Hello'.

When I am out shopping with Erin she thinks it's funny when strangers talk to me. Just the other day we were shopping in Bexhill and a man asked me to sign his baseball hat. It was a bit weird but I did. I suppose that's what you have to do when you are a celebrity.

The best thing about being famous is that people you don't even know give you things for free. One day Mum said I was going to get a surprise. I didn't know what to expect and thought maybe I was having a new game or new clothes or something. A big lorry pulled up outside the house and Mum said, 'The surprise is here.' I thought what can it be that it needs to come on a lorry? The surprise was wrapped in white plastic so I couldn't see what it was but it looked heavy because Dad had to help four men to carry it into the garden. Mum told me to go inside and helped me put on my bathers and my dressing gown. 'Is it a swimming pool?' I asked, but she said I would have to wait and see. Then we went back into the garden a man gave me a pair of scissors and told me I could open my surprise. I cut the wrapping and I could see it was wooden so I thought that maybe it was a new Wendy house. Mum and Dad helped me to pull off the plastic and I could see it was a big kajuzzi like the one I went in at the hospice but without the water. 'It's a hot tub of your very own,' Mum told me.

'Cool,' I said. I had to wait ages before I could use it because we had to fill it with water and a special liquid to keep my skin soft. When I got in it was lovely and warm like being in a big bath and the water squirted on my shoulders and my back. It felt lovely.

Mum explained that a lady had seen me on the television when I was in the kajuzzi at the hospice and it was her job to sell hot tubs. She said she wanted to give me one of my own because I loved them so much, so that's why I had it. I thanked the lady who brought it for me. It was a nice thing to do, I thought.

That's the thing about progeria, it has made me famous and that makes me happy. It's much better than having people staring and pointing at me.

Chapter 16
Kerry
Family Planning

I HAD ALWAYS DREAMED of a large family and desperately wanted Hayley to have brothers and sisters to grow up with. When doctors told us that the rare gene mutation causing progeria was not passed from parents to child and there would be a 95 per cent chance of having a normal baby after Hayley there was no medical reason not to. Or so I thought. Mark was not of the same opinion. After the initial shock of Hayley's condition, he had adapted to his role as dad to a progeria child but he wasn't keen to have more children.

A couple of weeks after we got back from our first trip to Disney World in 2000 I discovered I was pregnant. But it was not to be and I had a miscarriage after 10 weeks. It hit me for six. We'd just had our first scan photo and it was our baby so to have it taken away really hurt me emotionally. You would think after this close call we might have been more careful, but six months later I missed another period and again the pregnancy test showed a positive result. This time it was twins and again I lost them both – one at eight weeks and the second a fortnight later. The grief from both losses hit me hard, but I didn't feel I could talk to Mark. I worried that I would never be able to carry a normal, healthy child to full term.

Mark eventually came to understand how important another child was for me and we sat down and talked. For the first time in our relationship we had a conversation about family planning.

'I would like a son,' he admitted. 'One I can teach to play football and take to watch Chelsea play.' We sat around a calendar and worked out the best time for us both to have another child. We both agreed that we didn't want to miss out on the Progeria Reunions held every June. Some of the airlines refused to carry heavily pregnant women, so we decided that a May conception and a February birth would be the best time.

As we had already discovered our attempts at family planning were not the most successful. Within a few weeks of this conversation I missed a period and a test confirmed I was indeed expecting. It was September, I remember because I was sitting on the sofa waiting for the pregnancy test result and watching helplessly, along with the rest of the world as terrorists crashed two aeroplanes into the Twin Towers. I was given a due date of June 13 2002 – a week before the Progeria Reunion in Florida. Great timing again, I thought.

During my pregnancy my doctors took extra precautions and I was given scans at almost monthly intervals to check on the baby's progress. At 21 weeks, to Mark's delight, we were told it was a boy. I wanted to call him Lewis. It was a name I had always liked but Mark refused as Lewes, spelt differently but pronounced the same, was the name of a Sussex town just a few miles from where we lived. So we compromised and called him Louis.

When I told Hayley, 'Mummy is going to have a baby,' she was excited by the idea of having a younger sibling.

'Don't worry Mummy, I will help you look after him,' she said in the earnest way of a five year-old.

On June 18 2002, five days later than expected and after a 27-hour labour, Louis was born in the same hospital as Hayley. He was covered in jet black hair and weighed 7lb 14oz, 1lb 8oz heavier than his sister. When Mark brought Hayley in to hospital to see him for the first time she was fascinated by his thick black hair.

'Louis has brought you a little present to say hello,' I told her pointing to a small gift-wrapped box beside Louis' cot containing a DVD of the *Little Mermaid* film.

Hayley was thrilled and kissed the top of Louis' silky black head to say thank you. It was the start of a strong bond between brother and sister.

Back home, Hayley became Mummy's little helper. Whenever Louis cried to be changed, she would run off and bring me a clean nappy and nappy bag. And when he was being fed she would sit beside me as I breast fed him calling him a 'little piggy porker'. One thing was for sure, I never had any worries about Louis' growth. At every check up he gained a pound or two. Whereas Hayley never registered on the baby growth charts, Louis was following the 75 per cent arc of the percentile baby chart, meaning he was always way above average. I was a more relaxed mum too. After all the stress of Hayley's first years of life, I adopted a more laidback approach with our son. We were told there was no risk of him carrying the defective progeria gene and had full faith in the doctors. It was some years later that our Belgian friends the Vandeweerts proved science wrong with the birth of their second progeria child, Amber. So when Louis screamed with colic I wasn't overly worried. I would gently rock him in my arms and Hayley would sit beside me and stroke his head until he settled. At this time we were living in a three-bedroom house with Mark's youngest daughter Stacey, so space was at a premium. When Louis was old enough to sleep in his own bed, he moved in to share Hayley's pink bedroom.

Life continued as the perfect balanced family, then I missed another period. Once again my timing was all wrong. Louis was three, Mark was an out-of-work house-husband and I had gone back to college to study a course in reflexology and holistic medicine. Mark and I hadn't planned on having more children although deep in my heart I always hoped I would have more – just not at that particular time of my life when I was learning new skills with the intention of getting some part-time work as soon as Louis was old enough to start school to bring in some extra money. Again Mark was not happy (there was a pattern emerging here!) and we decided that after Ruby was born we wouldn't take any more risks and Mark booked to have a vasectomy.

When I told Hayley we would be having another baby in the house, she was excited but a bit concerned where the new addition would sleep. When I told her, 'We're moving to a new house where you can have a bedroom each,' she was happy enough. 'I hope it's a girl so we can play together,' she said. Sure enough when the scan showed I was having another girl, Hayley was over the moon and planned all the games she would play with her new sister. We decided we would call her Katy. 'I can call her Kit Kat,' Hayley said. But Mark hated the name and we reached a stalemate. Hayley and I were convinced we would win Mark around but he refused to budge. Then a couple of weeks before I went into labour we were all watching the TV soap *EastEnders* when the character Ruby walked onto Albert Square.

'What about Ruby?' said Mark. So Ruby it was.

Throughout the pregnancy Hayley loved touching and kissing my swollen tummy and would often sit beside me and sing nursery rhymes into my belly to feel little Ruby moving. Hayley had also started learning to play the violin in school and was convinced that Ruby would like to listen to her practising. Whenever she played Ruby would move inside me, but I think she was just trying to get away from the screeching noise of Hayley's beginner's violin scales. Carrying Ruby for nine months was bliss. I knew that it would be the last time I would be pregnant, given our belated family planning scheme, and I wanted to enjoy every last moment from the late-night craving for chocolate Minstrels to the healthy glow of my skin that made my friends and family say, 'You look well.' When I was carrying Louis, I ballooned. I was so huge I could hardly walk in the last few weeks and I could just about manage to waddle to the bathroom. But Ruby was a joy, I was much smaller and I hardly felt like I was pregnant.

I felt the healthiest I had been in my life.

On June 2 2005, after an eight-hour labour, Ruby was born and turned out to be the biggest of all our babies weighing 8lb 2oz. She was delivered by the same midwife who had brought Hayley into the world eight years earlier and after all that time she still remembered Hayley's big blue eyes – once seen never forgotten, I always say. Ruby had dark eyes and a thick layer of hair. Like Louis she was a healthy baby. Immediately our family life changed to accommodate the new addition. We moved into a larger four-bedroom council house across the road from where we lived, Stacey moved out to live with her mother and Hayley and Louis had their own bedrooms. We had been busy decorating our new home and for the first time we had space for a proper nursery. Once again Hayley proved she was would make a great mum, she would sit on the sofa with Ruby on her lap singing nursery rhymes and

Kylie songs as she gently rocked her to sleep.

As Louis and Ruby grew up and became more independent, the fights started between Hayley and her brother and sister. When Ruby started to get a mind of her own, she learnt how to annoy her older siblings. It was quite common for Ruby or Louis to come crying to me because Hayley had hurt them. As her younger brother and sister started to tower over her, Hayley learnt that the only way she could hurt them was to pinch their cheeks. She couldn't lash out and punch or kick like they could because she would just fall over and end up hurting herself, so the cheek-pinch became her effective method of fighting back. When fights erupted, quite often out of nothing more than Ruby's refusal to let Hayley be the boss or Louis not allowing one of his sisters to play on his Xbox games console, I would stand back and let them get on with it, knowing it would eventually end in tears. Even now there are some nights when Ruby will creep into my bedroom while Hayley and Louis are asleep, and start to cry. 'I've been nasty to Hayley, what if something bad happens to her.' It's a terrible thing for a six-year-old to carry that weight of responsibility. 'That's why you should always be nice to one another,' I tell her and the message sinks in for a day or so. The next morning Ruby apologises to Hayley and gives her a big hug and everything is fine, until the next time ...

As parents Mark and I have had to maintain the balance to share our time and affection between the children. Both Ruby and Louis know that Hayley's progeria makes her different from them and they seem to accept it. I have been known to buy Hayley extra little presents when she has to have difficult treatment and they understand that this comes from her own moneybox which is topped up from her publicity fees, and although young they seem to understand this. For me the hardest part is saying no to Hayley when she wants to go shopping for new clothes or gadgets. In my heart I want to give her everything she asks for because I know that I will not have the chance when she is older. But sometimes I have to say no as there's a fine line between being a special child and a spoilt brat.

Hayley and Ruby would often sit together and watch Disney DVDs, they loved the sugar candy pinkness and happy-ever-after of classics like Beauty and the Beast and Cinderella. I don't know whether this gave Hayley any ideas, but one day she turned to Mark and I as we were cuddling on the sofa in one of our rarer loving moments , and said, 'If two people love each other, they should get married.' Mark and I were slightly shocked. The idea of marriage had never been a priority to us. Sure when I was a kid, like Hayley, I had dreamed of a fairytale wedding with a big church and a crowd of hundreds watching me walk down the aisle to the Wedding March. But the older I got I realised that fairytales are just that and our priority as parents was to take care of our children and find a cure for Hayley's condition. A wedding seemed like an unnecessary expense. But Hayley had planted the seed of the idea. In her mind she wanted her 'big day' and the only way she was likely to do that was through Mark and me.

The more I thought about it, marriage seemed to make sense. Hayley and Louis were both at an age where having parents with different surnames, although not uncommon, needed some explanation. Louis and Hayley were often puzzled when their teachers gave them letters addressed to 'Mrs Button'. So Mark and I set a date and a place – July 29 2006 at Hastings Register Office – and I started arranging our big day with Hayley as my assistant wedding planner. Hayley had it all mapped out in her head. She and

Ruby would be bridesmaids and they would be wearing pink, of course. There would be a pink cravat for Daddy, his best man and Louis, the pageboy.

The wedding itself was going to have to be a low-key affair, we didn't have thousands of pounds to waste on a lavish party. I didn't even have a spare couple of hundred pounds to buy a wedding dress. Fortunately a local wedding dress shop heard about the plans and offered to donate Hayley a bridesmaid's dress for her big day. They also allowed me to buy my dress and Ruby's at cost price. So, before 'austerity weddings' became fashionable, Mark and I had our own budget-busting ceremony for just 25 close family and friends. I chose a two-piece skirt and bustière top in ivory silk made in Paris. Hayley got her wishes – a beautiful cerise pink chiffon dress, which matched the pink crystals on my dress but it had to be altered several times before it fitted her tiny frame. On the morning of the wedding Hayley took charge helping her brother and sister into their outfits. Louis was our page boy and wore a suit with a pink cravat to match his Daddy's and little Ruby wore a baby pink dress. After the ceremony Hayley paraded around wearing my veil saying, 'Look at me, Mum. I'm the bride.' It broke my heart to see her and think she would never grow up to have a wedding of her own.

After the ceremony my mum took the kids and my brother and sister for a post-wedding lunch at a local pub while a limo arrived to drive Mark and I to our honeymoon destination – a rave festival. We headed to Warwickshire to spend our first night as husband and wife at the Global Gathering festival, doing what we loved most – dancing with a group of 10 cousins and friends. Most couples go for a slow smooch first dance, but ours was a full-on, glowsticks-in-the-air rave that lasted until dawn with

45,000 other people. Not the typical wedding, some might say, but ours wasn't a typical romance.

Chapter 17
Hayley
Sibling Rivalry

I WAS NOT PLEASED when my brother Louis was born. I had to share my bedroom with him and he would wake me up in the middle of the night crying. When my sister Ruby was born I was happy. I wanted a sister to play with and I knew when she was old enough we could share our dolls and clothes. When I was little I had loads of Bratz dolls and I would let Ruby play with them and I would do her make-up. Now I am too old to play with Bratz and Ruby doesn't let me do her make-up any more. I asked her why but she just says she doesn't want to. I think I may have done it wrong once, but I don't really know.

Me and Ruby have a weird relationship. Sometimes we hate each other and other times we are best friends. It depends what mood Ruby is in. If she's in a bad mood we hate each other. We argue a lot. But at the end of an argument Ruby says, 'Are we still best friends, Hayley?' I say, 'Yes we're still best friends, Ruby,' until the next time when we argue again. When my best friend Erin comes round to hang out with me, Ruby decides she wants me to do her make-up and I say no, go away because I am busy. Recently Ruby has started saying, 'You don't love me Hayley,' when I tell her to go away. I say, 'Don't use that excuse.' But I still feel bad when she comes into my room crying and hugs me. I think she might get jealous of my friends.

Sometimes Ruby can be really annoying. Like once we were out in the garden playing with our tea set and I went to pour some juice in Ruby's cup but she wanted to pour the juice. I told her to say please. She didn't say please so I wouldn't let her have the juice. She ran in the house to tell Mum. That was really annoying. I hate snitches and I hate it when Ruby is a snitch. Sometimes I wish Mum would have another baby sister but one that would let me put make-up on her and won't snitch. Louis annoys me when he won't let me watch my programmes on TV or he won't let me play on his Xbox.

I feel like Ruby and Louis' big sister even though Louis is taller than me and Ruby is almost as tall as me. I ask them about their day at school and help them out with their homework. When I am watching TV in my room Ruby usually comes in and asks if I will help her. Sometimes I do, but it depends what mood I'm in and what I'm watching on TV. When I say no she always cries.

At night before we go to sleep me and Louis talk about random stuff. I tell him when I have aches in my body and he says, 'I'm really glad I don't have progeria.' Other times Louis worries that he is the smallest in his class. I told him, 'Don't worry, Louis, I am the littlest in the whole school, just deal with it.' Louis has a girlfriend now and it's really sweet. When I ask him about his girlfriend he goes all shy. I don't have a boyfriend, I'm not interested in boys they smell and they are annoying and they expect you to do the washing up. Louis is a typical boy, he just sits around watching TV. Daddy is not annoying and he smells nice but he doesn't do the washing up. Mum says I have a boyfriend called Harry, but he is not my boyfriend. He's just a friend. He is eleven years old and lives in Yorkshire with his mum Sharron. He has progeria as well but his is a different sort of progeria. He ages five times faster. I met Harry when Mum took me to London on the TV programme *This Morning* and he was really nice and funny. We talk on Facebook all the time. Mum says he is a 'real gentleman'.

I think Ruby sometimes get jealous of me. One day when someone was filming me for TV, she wanted to get in front of the camera and the people with the camera asked her to play in the other room. She said, 'Why do they always want to film Hayley and not me?' Mum told her it's because I have progeria. If Ruby gets jealous, she goes off to play with her friends and forgets about it.

I can understand why she feels that way, if it was reversed I would be asking exactly the same thing and be acting the same. Louis doesn't act like Ruby, but he doesn't like getting his picture taken so every time the cameras come he hides in his room and plays on his Xbox.

Sometimes I feel jealous of Ruby. I'm not sure why. She has really nice clothes and I used to be able to steal them from her wardrobe. But now she is getting taller than me. Every day she says, 'Hayley let's see how tall we are?' She makes a really big deal that she's taller than me. So I usually stand on my tiptoes, when we measure so I look taller. I don't feel jealous of Ruby and Louis' health. If I didn't have progeria, I would not get to do cool stuff and meet really cool people.

Chapter 18
Kerry
The Second Worst Day of my Life

HAYLEY'S CLOSEST FRIEND – THE one who understood her the most was Maddie. Maddie was three years older than Hayley but they had so much in common apart from their progeria. We first met Maddie and her family at one of the early Progeria Reunions in America and when we both returned to our homes in the UK, we stayed in touch and met up often so the girls could have sleepovers.

They would play together for hours, painting one another's finger nails and putting make-up on each other's faces.

One Sunday afternoon after Maddie had returned home from one of their sleepovers I had a frantic phone call telling me Maddie had been rushed to hospital. I arrived at the emergency unit to be told the news. Maddie had suffered a massive heart attack and had passed away. She was just eleven years old.

My heart was in pieces for Maddie's mum. There were no words I could say that would change anything. I tried to put myself in her place and imagined how I would be feeling. It was too horrible to think about. And worst of all I had to go home and break the news to Hayley. How could I tell her that her best friend, the one person in the world she was closest to and had most in common with, was no longer with us? When I had left our house earlier that afternoon Hayley had no idea Maddie had been taken ill.

As I turned the key in the front door lock, I could feel my heart throbbing in my mouth. I took a deep breath, trying to compose myself for the task ahead, and walked into the living room where Hayley was watching her favourite cartoon Spongebob Squarepants. Fighting back the tears, I switched off the TV and sat down beside Hayley and that's when the floodgates opened.

'What's the matter, Mummy?' Hayley asked as she climbed onto my lap. Sensing that something bad had happened she started to rub my cheek, just like she had done the day five years ago when the doctor delivered the news about her progeria.

'Mummy has been with Maddie because she wasn't feeling very well,' I said, choking back the tears.

'We had to get an ambulance for her. Mummy went over to hospital with her. But she was too tired and she went to sleep and she's gone to Heaven.'

I didn't need to say any more. Hearing the word Heaven, Hayley burst into uncontrollable sobs. I wrapped my arms around her, drawing her tight to my chest. 'It hurts in my tummy, Mummy. My heart really hurts,' she cried.

Apart from the day when we had confirmation of Hayley's progeria, Maddie's death was the second most upsetting time for our family. As the parent of a progeria child death is something that is always in the back of your mind. When we looked back over the old photographs taken at the Progeria Reunions Mark and I would add up the number of children no longer with us and count our blessings that we still had Hayley. But Maddie's passing was more devastating because the girls had been so close and spent so much time together.

The hardest decision was whether we should let Hayley go to the funeral. She was only eight and while we wanted to do what was best for her, we didn't want her to start worrying about death. But Hayley wanted to go. Not knowing how to deal with such a delicate issue, we deferred to Hayley's care worker Jane, who suggested it would be therapeutic for Hayley to attend.

'Can I wear my purple dress? Because pink and purple were Maddie's favourite colours.' Hayley asked.

Hayley sat down at her computer and wrote a letter to her friend that she wanted to read to her at the funeral. On the day of the funeral Hayley coped better than we had expected. She stood up in front of a crowded church, where everyone wore pink and purple in honour of Maddie. When she read her letter to Maddie there wasn't a dry eye in the church. In the cemetery Mark and I stood beside the open grave holding Hayley's hand, she bent down and placed a card and her favourite photograph of the two of them on top of the coffin, as it was lowered into the ground.

In the weeks that followed Maddie's funeral Hayley would regularly talk about Maddie. She said she had seen her in her dreams. We would sit down together and draw her pictures and write letters. For a while she had an obsession about visiting Maddie's grave. I would take her to the grave yard and she would lay letters and little bracelets beside the headstone which was shaped like Piglet from the Winnie the Pooh books. She bought a wind chime to hang in the tree beside Maddie's grave and placed a tiny grey fairy on top of the ground above the grave to watch over her friend. Other days she would ask if she could visit Maddie's house and sit in her bedroom taking presents and pictures to place on her bed and cards to stick on the wall. Her letters to Maddie usually had a picture of Piglet on top.

One read: 'Dear Maddie, I just want to say I miss you a lot and everyone says, "hello Maddie". It's really annoying. Must go now. Love Hayley.'

During this distressing time, Hayley's counsellor Jane was invaluable. It was not always easy to have difficult discussions with Hayley as she tried to protect us from her true feelings and fears. But when she was painting and drawing or making things with Jane, she seemed to open up and talk about Maddie's death and her own life expectancy. Jane also introduced us to *Muddles, Puddles and Sunshine*, a book which helped young children cope with bereavement. It told the story of two characters called Bee and the Bear and there were puzzles and games to help Hayley to make sense of her feelings of loss. 'She has a very positive attitude towards Maddie's death and is comfortable with it,' Jane relayed back to us a week or so after the funeral. 'Clearly she has put Maddie in a beautiful place. When she thinks of her, she pictures her in heaven, she has hair and she is dressed up in beautiful clothes. Hayley feels she can go and visit her in her dreams. She can put herself in the dream with her and she's comfortable.'

Maddie's death was, without a doubt, the most traumatic thing to happen to Hayley. For although her life had been one long succession of hospital appointments, poking, prodding and pills, it had been outweighed by the happy times: hobnobbing with the stars and visiting the kinds of exotic places most of her friends had never heard of. Yet no matter what she did, Maddie's name was always in her conversations. It was as if by talking about her, she was keeping her memory alive. One afternoon, while we were out shopping, Hayley came out with something that stopped me in my tracks. We had just reached the front door of Matalan, when Hayley said, 'Mum, Maddie's just whispered in my ear. She was going "Hey, Hay, can I come shopping with you."'

Oh my God, is she really hearing voices? I thought. I didn't want to discourage her, so I replied, 'Of course, she can come along, Chick. And she can help you choose a necklace if you like.' Inside the shop, she chose two identical angel necklaces: one for her and one for Maddie which she placed in her bedroom.

The hardest part of Maddie's death was the knowledge that there was a treatment in sight. Two months earlier we had been at the Progeria Reunion in America when Dr Leslie Gordon from the Progeria Research Foundation told us of a new treatment they were working on. It broke my heart knowing that we were so close to the breakthrough we have been waiting for all our lives and Maddie never lived to get the chance to try it.

Chapter 19
Hayley
My First Funeral

I HAD NEVER BEEN to a funeral before until I went to Maddie's. Maddie was my best friend. She was nearly four years older than me but we were like sisters. Some people even thought we were really sisters. We used to give each other presents all of the time. Once she gave me a teddy bear holding a heart that said 'Sisters are really angels in disguise'. We liked angels.

Maddie didn't really mind about her progeria, and neither did I when I was with her. When we were together we acted as if we didn't have it.

The last time I saw Maddie was the day before she died. We had a sleepover at my house and we argued over my Nintendo DS. She wanted to play on it and I didn't want her to because I wanted her to play with me. We had a bit of an argument.

The next morning, after Maddie had gone home, Mummy got called away. I didn't know where she had gone, but she rushed out suddenly. When I asked my dad he said it was 'grown-up' stuff. That usually means that it's something boring, so I sat down and watched TV.

It was hours before Mum came home and when she did I noticed her eyes were red as if she had been crying. She turned off the TV while I was watching SpongeBob

SquarePants. It was one I had seen before where SpongeBob can't stop laughing and Squidward gets really annoyed. Why are you turning the telly off? I thought, then Mum sat next to me and started crying. She said Maddie had gone to heaven. That made me so sad. I started crying too. I sat on Mummy's lap and we both cried and cried. I cried so much that my tummy started to hurt.

One day after Maddie had gone I heard Mummy and Daddy talking about going to Maddie's funeral.

'What's a funeral?' I asked. They said it was when people go to a grave yard before they go up to heaven. I remembered I had been to the grave yard with Nanna and Pops so I said I wanted to go to the grave yard with Maddie, too.

Mummy wasn't very happy about it. She said it would be better if I stayed home with Nanna and Pops.

'But I want to say sorry to Maddie,' I said. They said I could go as long as I wouldn't get upset.

The night before the funeral I sat in my bedroom and wrote a card to my friend. I traced a photo of Piglet because she liked Piglet.

For the funeral I wore my purple satin dress, Mummy wore a pink top, and Daddy wore a pink tie. That's what Maddie would have liked. She didn't like black. She wanted people to wear pink and purple. I knew this because we talked about it. Mum said I could put some make-up on to go and she let me choose what colour eye shadow I wanted to wear. I chose purple to match my dress. I wanted to wear Mummy's wedding veil, but she said that was a bit much.

At the church Maddie's mummy and sisters were crying all the time. I cried a little bit too. There was a man in black with a white collar around his neck, reading from a book, he said lots of nice things about Maddie and her progeria. Then I was allowed to say the speech I had written.

I said, 'Maddie, I love you lots and always. I'm sorry we had a fight. Thank you for being my best friend and sister. Hope you had a safe journey. See you in Heaven. P.S. Have fun.'

I felt sad and upset, but I didn't cry. Mummy and Daddy were crying and lots of Maddie's aunties and uncles and cousins were crying too.

When I went to bed that night I dreamt about Maddie. In my dream we didn't have progeria because we had taken a cure. We both had hair. My friend was tall with long, blonde hair. She looked like a normal eleven-year-old girl. In the dream I was out shopping. I went up to the counter and Maddie was an angel. She said to me, 'Hello Hayley. See? I'm not really dead.'

I always talk about Maddie as I don't want her to ever be forgotten. In my bedroom I have a memory box where I keep all of the things I don't want to throw away like birthday cards, old photos and tickets from our trips to America. In my box I also keep a half eaten packet of crunched-up Frazzles that Maddie didn't finish on her last sleepover. Maddie's teeth were not very strong so she couldn't crunch crisps. Whenever we had crisps I would squash them into little bits for her so that she could eat them. She had kept half the packet for the next day, but she never had the chance to eat them.

I miss Maddie the most when I am sad or hurting. I think she was the only one who could understand what I am going through. Sometimes when I wish hard enough I can hear her. She says, 'Hello, Hay,' that's what she used to call me. I am never sure whether I really hear her voice or if I am dreaming, but it sounds real to me. One day I hope I will see Maddie again in Heaven.

Chapter 20
Kerry
Hope for Hayley

FOR CHRISTMAS 2005 MARK and I took Hayley, Louis and baby Ruby on holiday to Disney World, Florida, to meet up with Dr Leslie Gordon and Scott Berns, founders of the Progeria Research Foundation, and their son, Sam. A year older than Hayley, Sam was a happy, all-American school boy who loved Lego and the Boy Scouts.

As we were standing beside the tea cup ride, watching Hayley, Louis and Sam spinning around and laughing, Leslie said the words we had been so desperate to hear,

'I think we might be close to starting a drug trial.' Although it was unofficial and still under wraps it was the best Christmas present we could have wished for. I looked across to Hayley and Sam, who were grinning as the force of the spinning tea cup rocked them from side to side. Was it too much to dream that these children would live to an age where one day they would be seeking their thrills from white-knuckle roller-coasters instead of gentle merry-go-round rides?

For the past four years Leslie and a team of scientists in America had been trying to find the cause of progeria in order to work on a cure. Every year at the Progeria Reunions, parents would get an update on the laboratory work and we would go home and cross our fingers, hoping that one day in Hayley's lifetime a drug would be found to counteract the devastating effects of progeria. By taking samples from children at the reunions, Leslie and The Progeria Research Foundation had built up a cell bank that held the progeria cells for scientists to discover things like the gene mutation which caused progeria. In 2003 they had come up with an exciting breakthrough discovery. They had found that the reason children like Hayley were ageing so quickly was all down to a tiny mutation in each child's DNA. Every human cell has a protein called Lamin A, which holds the nucleus of the cell together, but they found that progeria children had a defective mutation in their Lamin A called progerin. Progerin was a defective and unstable protein that caused children to age prematurely and only one in eight million children were affected by it.

'We now know enough about progerin to find a potential treatment for it,' Leslie explained. 'We have found a drug called farnesyltransferase inhibitor. We treated cells with it and also progeria mice with it and it looks promising in those experiments. Now we have to wait for approval from the American Federal Government's Drug Agency to start human clinical trials.'

I wanted to hug her. With every year that passed more children died and it became more urgent that a cure could be found in time for Hayley. Our once naïve notion that a pill could combat Hayley's condition now seemed to be more real. But the question remained – would it arrive in Hayley's life time? Our holiday ended on a high and we flew home to Britain to wait for the call that we hoped would change our lives for ever.

As part of the ongoing research, we were asked if Hayley would be willing to take part in a major study into progeria which was being carried out at the National Institute of Health in Maryland, near Washington DC.

Once the scientists working with the Progeria Research Foundation had discovered the progeria gene in 2002 they knew they would need to understand progeria at a clinical level if they were ever going to find a cure. In order to do this the PRF had teamed up with researchers at the NIH to launch the Natural History Study to get a better insight into the bodies of progeria children. A total of 15 children, including Hayley, were invited to take part in the tests. It meant two week-long trips to the US for a full body MOT. Everything was tested and checked; height, weight, heart, blood, bones and teeth. They even tested her tears for acidity using litmus paper. They also made her walk on a treadmill to test her heart rate under strain. During these tests Hayley became the first progeria child to complete an MRI scan to build up a picture of the inside of her body. Usually children of that age were unable to lie still for long enough to get a complete picture, but Hayley managed to spend 45 minutes in complete darkness to give doctors their first insight into the body of these special children. During these tests doctors noticed a constriction in one of the arteries in her neck which was feeding her brain. It was a worry as strokes were one of the common killers of progeria children, but we were able to monitor it and it righted itself in time.

After the Washington tests, we returned home and waited and waited. Winter turned to spring, and there was still no news. Summer came and we flew to America for another reunion, but there was still no start date. With every week that passed we became more frustrated. We were told that the treatment had been tested on mice and the early results were promising. The mice had put on weight and lived longer. I understood that the US Government's Drug Agency had to give its approval before they could be allowed to test the drug on children, but a clock in my head was ticking. Time was not on our side. Every month we waited was almost a year off Hayley's short life. The wheels of government might move slowly, but progeria doesn't.

In the meantime Mark registered a charity in Hayley's name to raise money to support children and their families living with progeria. With Mark as chairman, me as vice-chairman and a family friend as trustee, Hayley's Hope gathered the numerous offers of help with fundraising and donations from well-wishers into a central charity, which helped to pay for extra expenses for our trips to Boston, which weren't being covered by the Progeria Research Foundation. Through the charity we were also able to donate money to the foundation for their on-going research.

On April 28 2007, we finally had the official call we had been waiting for. Hayley had been accepted on to the drug trial. I remember the day well as our Belgian friends, the Vandeweerts, who had been frequent visitors to our home since our first meeting at the Progeria Reunion, were on the final day of a holiday with us in England. Hayley and Michiel were playing in the garden, I was in the kitchen cooking pasta for our dinner when the phone rang. It was Leslie.

'Great news. We've had the go-ahead from the Drug Agency. The trials are starting next week,' she said. Sixteen months of anticipation were over, 28 children from 16 countries would soon be flown out to Boston Children's Hospital, two at a time, to be given what we hoped would be the wonder drug. They would start with some of the American children. Hayley was being paired up with her friend Michiel for her treatment, which would start on May 26. It meant that for the next two years we were committing ourselves to fly out to Boston every four months, for a total of seven visits.

Leslie explained that arrangements were being made for Hayley and Michiel to spend five days at the children's hospital. For the first four days she would have every test and scan available to ensure her ageing body was capable of taking the new drug. Then on the last day she would be given the pill, making history as the first child from the UK to test it. In the meantime we had already spoken to our own doctors in the UK, who consented to monitor Hayley on a weekly basis checking for growth and improvement and potential side-effects. Their health reports would then be fed back to the research team in Boston.

'Are we doing the right thing, taking part in this trial?' I asked Mark. 'This drug has never been tested on humans before. We don't know if it will work or if it will cause more damage.' We had been warned about the possible side-effects which ranged from mild nausea on one end of the scale to possible death at the other end.

'Without it the prognosis is not good, so we have no choice, really,' Mark said.

He was right. Without the drug we were four years away from the dreaded life expectancy age of thirteen. For every year after that we would be living on borrowed time, worrying that at any moment Hayley could suddenly drop and pass away in our arms, just like her friend Maddie.

'There are side-effects for everything. Even paracetamol can cause breathing difficulties in some extreme cases if you read the small print. The drug companies are just covering themselves. We have to look on the positive side. We can't let Hayley sense we are worried,' Mark said. I knew he was right, but it wasn't easy to follow his advice. My mum had also been putting a dampener on it ever since we first mentioned the possible trials a year earlier.

'What if it goes wrong?' she asked.

'I know it's a risk because the drugs have never been used on progeria children before,' I replied. 'But we know what the best outcome could be – a longer and healthier life for Hayley. We just don't know what the side-effects will be, if any. She's getting older, Mum. It's a risk I'm willing to take. We have no choice.' I reassured her that we were in safe hands as the drug company was one of the biggest in the world. 'They are not going to play God with our children,' I continued. But I understood Mum's concerns, I had already spent many nights lying awake worrying about the consequences if it went wrong.

In the days leading up to our departure for Boston, I began to sense that Hayley might be getting nervous. One night as I tucked her into bed and kissed her goodnight, she asked, 'Can we delay the trial, Mummy?' Waiting was no longer an option, but how could I tell a nine-year-old child that her life is so fragile we may not have the opportunity next year?

Instead I replied, 'We've got our plane tickets and hotel all booked, we can't change the dates now. And Michiel will be disappointed if you don't go, he's looking forward to seeing you again.' I was aware that Hayley was afraid of sharing worries with Mark and me. She worried that she might upset us. I was apprehensive too, but I had to put on an optimistic face for everyone's sake.

The night before our first trip to Boston we threw a 'good luck' party with all of our family and Hayley's friends at a local pub, the White Rock Hotel. 'Can I wear make-up, Mum?' Hayley asked as she picked out her outfit for the night – a white flowery dress and matching headscarf. I let her choose the colour of her eyeshadow. 'Pink to match the flowers on my scarf,' she said. She was growing up into such a girlie girl, she had her own sense of style and fashion. At eleven some people might have said she was too young to be dressing up in make-up when she was pretty enough without it. But my attitude was always to let her be. She might never reach an age when she can go out for a night on the town independently, so I wanted her to enjoy her life.

A long, black stretch limo pulled up outside our house to chauffeur Hayley round the corner to her party where all of her aunties, uncles, cousins, friends from school and their parents were waiting. She danced the Locomotion and the Macarena, she ate sandwiches and crisps, and she spent the night telling everyone how excited she was to be going to America. When the party ended, Mark took over the DJ's microphone and thanked everyone for coming.

'Keep your fingers crossed when we're out in America and we will do our best to come back with some good news.'

All our friends raised their crossed fingers in the air in unison and cheered. 'Good luck, Hayley!' We didn't know what lay ahead. We had nothing to lose, but, in a way, we had everything to lose.

Chapter 21
Hayley
I'm Gonna Grow Hair

ONE DAY MUM SAID to me that they had found some tablets that might cure progeria and she asked if I wanted some. I was really excited and said to myself, 'You're gonna grow hair. You're gonna grow tall.'

'Will I have to have needles?' I asked. I hate needles. Even if the doctors put stuff on my skin to make it go numb first, I still don't like them. I always have to have needles for blood tests and stuff. But Mum said it would just be tablets, so I said that would be all right. Here we go again, that means there will probably be needles, I thought.

Mum explained that we would have to go to a hospital in America if I wanted to have the tablets. I thought that was a long way to go just to get tablets. We usually get them from the chemist in town. I had been to America for the Progeria Reunions and when we went on holiday to Disney World and stuff but going to America to go to the hospital was different. Mum said that the tablets were very special and hadn't been given to many children with progeria before and I would be one of the first. That made me feel really special.

Before I could have the drug I had to have an MRI scan to take pictures of the inside of my whole body. It was really scary, like going into a big tunnel. I couldn't lift my arm or move or anything and I had to lie still for 45 minutes. When I went into the tunnel only my foot was sticking out of the end. Mum held on to it and I said, 'If I shake my foot, I want to come out.' Inside the scanner there were little things on my chest to hold me down. At first it was like being in a dark tunnel and the loud bangs sounded like someone trying to get in. It was scary, but exciting. I thought to myself, at least I'm not having needles and if I don't do it I will be ill and I could possibly die. So I just thought of all the positive stuff and tried to be still. I was so still I almost fell asleep. The doctors said it was the first time a child had stayed still for 45 minutes. Other children were moving too much. I told them I had fallen asleep and they laughed. If I could I would make it so that there were no noisy machines and no needles. But I can't, and that's OK.

At first I didn't really think too much about what the trial meant because I was still quite little. I just thought, let's go for it. Mum and Dad were worrying about it and making all the decisions. But I was too little to understand. Some days I could tell they were really worried. They didn't have to say anything, but I could tell. When I saw they were scared I wondered why they were so worried. What's the worst thing it could do? I could get really poorly. The best thing that could happen would be if I was just like a normal kid. One day I overheard Mum on the phone to Nanna and she was crying. I thought it must be something really bad. Later that night when Mum was tucking me up in bed I said, 'Can we go to America another time?' But she said we had to go because everything was booked and the doctors would be waiting to see us. Then she said I would get to see Michiel and his mum and dad and sister, Amber, and that cheered me up. I was looking forward to seeing them. Michiel is just crazy.

Whenever we used to see him at the reunions he was always hyper and running around, and he speaks good English.

Before we went to Boston for the first time Mum and Dad threw a party for all my friends to say goodbye. It was good fun and I ran around and played. Everyone was giving me presents and saying good luck, which was nice of them. But when we left everyone was crying. I thought that maybe they were crying because they weren't sure what was going to happen and whether the drugs would work. Then I thought to myself it must be all right, Mum and Dad would not let me go on the trial if it was going to be dangerous. But when everyone was crying I started to get a bit nervous, and I thought, what if something went wrong?

The night before we left I had a dream. In my dream I took the drug and woke up and had really long hair and was really tall. I looked like my sister Ruby. It was a cool time. When I woke up I remember thinking, that's what's going to happen, your hair is going to grow. But I knew it wouldn't happen overnight.

Chapter 22
Kerry
Boston Drug Trials

MAY 19 2007: ALMOST 400 years after the first English settlers founded Boston, Massachusetts, Mark, Hayley, Louis and I arrived in the city to create our own little piece of medical history. It was amazing to think that in seven years scientific progress had advanced so quickly on progeria and Hayley would soon be the first child from England to try out the new miracle drug farnesyltransferase inhibitor, or FTI for short. We were well aware that Hayley was being used as a human guinea pig but to be given the chance to prolong her life was beyond anything we had ever wished for.

After a seven-hour flight we were all exhausted and couldn't wait to check into our hotel. I carried Hayley through Boston's Logan Airport while Louis, who was only four at the time, slept in his daddy's arms. We had arrived two days early to give us all the weekend to recover from the jetlag and calm our nerves before the trial started. Travelling with the Vandeweert family meant we had been able to take our minds off the uncertainty that lay ahead. For two days we were European tourists on vacation. We rode the green and orange Old Town trolley bus around the city, taking in all the sights, from the aquarium to the famous Boston Red Sox baseball stadium.

On the Monday morning we arrived at Boston Children's Hospital, which would be our home for the next five days. We checked into our family room at a nearby hotel and took the shuttle bus to the hospital to meet Dr Mark Kieran, director of paediatric medical neuro-oncology at the hospital. He had extensive experience with the FTI drug in children and was leading the team of 28 medics and scientists working on the progeria drug trial. It was crazy to think that in just four years, through their exhaustive efforts, the Progeria Research Foundation's research team had not only discovered the gene that caused progeria but had found a drug that might work to slow down the ageing process. They had also raised enough money to fund the costs of the trials including the travel, food and lodging expenses for the 28 families taking part.

Before we could start any tests we had to sit down with the doctors and scientists leading the trial to make sure that we understood everything that the trial involved. There were risks and benefits. By being given the drugs, which could save Hayley's life, we were also agreeing to follow their strictly confidential guidelines and sign a legal document showing that we were agreeing to take part in the trial with our eyes open. At that point, when the doctors handed us a thirty-page consent form to sign, we realised the seriousness of the process we were entering. Once again we were given the list of the possible side-effects, which ranged from mild nausea to heart attack and possibly death. The trials were not something we had entered blindly, but seeing everything spelled out in black and white and our signatures on the bottom meant that there was no going back. It was scary but also strangely uplifting to think that this could be the cure we had prayed for. We were putting all our hopes in the hands of these doctors; who admitted that they didn't know with any certainty what would happen.

The doctors tried their best to explain to us how they expected the new drugs would work. Progeria was caused when a 'bad' molecule called a 'farnesyl group' attached itself to the progerin protein and stopped the cell from working properly. The FTIs would act as a barrier, stopping the progerin from damaging the cells and slowing down the ageing characteristics of progeria. It wasn't only children like Hayley who could benefit from this group of drugs. We were told that drug companies had spent the last 10 years and millions of pounds developing FTIs that they hoped one day would cure cancer. Although cancers were caused by very different proteins they were using the same principle that the drug could block the path of the cancer-causing protein.

Before Hayley could take the drug she had to have a full MOT to make sure her 'seventy-five-year-old' body was strong enough to cope. We presented the doctors with our daily weight and food diary, which we had been asked to keep during the month before the trial date. They noted her weight and height against the chart. She weighed 12kgs and was 97cm tall. The average nine-year-old girl should weigh double that and be at least 30cm taller. As she lay on a bed looking helpless, naked except for the hospital regulation paper pants, the nurses tested her heart with an ECG then fitted a clip on her finger tip to check the oxygen levels in her blood.

Once the tests came back positive, it was time for Hayley to take this 'wonder drug'. It was the final day of our visit and we were taken into a room. Doctors and nurses were there, waiting to give Hayley her first shot at a longer life. It was an historic occasion; she was the first child in Europe, and only the third child in the world, to test the drug. We sat her down beside a table, where the white capsule was laid out ready. Beside it was a paper cup filled with water. Mark had his video camera running, recording every magic moment, and one of the hospital nurses had her camera ready too. Hayley smiled, holding the pill bottle in her hand. Then, with no hesitation, she picked up the pill and popped it in her mouth. Against the frailness of her tiny, bony fingers the pill looked enormous. With both hands she picked up the paper cup and took a big gulp of water. We stood nervously watching and holding our breath. Hayley's little cheeks puffed out with the water and her eyes grew wide. 'Big mouthfuls of drink,' I shouted in encouragement, thinking she was about to choke.

Just as I felt the panic rising inside me, she opened her mouth wide and grinned for the flashing cameras. History had been made. We now had to wait to see what effect it would have.

We flew home two days later with a suitcase full of pill bottles, enough to cover her daily dose of one pill in the morning and one pill at night for the next four months. But as soon as we arrived home the side-effects started. Hayley got up the next morning and said she didn't want any breakfast as she was feeling sick. I looked at Mark, terror was written all over his face. Was this the start of something really serious? Panic set in and I got on the phone to Boston Children's Hospital to find out what to do. They prescribed Zofran, a drug which is used for patients undergoing chemotherapy. Mark rushed down to our pharmacist to collect the drugs. The sooner we could give her them, the quicker they would make her feel better. For the rest of the day she lay in bed, too weak to be bothered with anything or anyone. Mark and I asked ourselves, had we made the biggest mistake of our lives?

I wasn't aware of it at the time, but we must have gone

into nostalgia mode. Mark and I found ourselves watching old home videos of Hayley just after her diagnosis. In the film she was splashing around in her little paddling pool in the garden, her hair was swept back over her head in a big brown quiff. She seemed so happy and carefree, unlike the frail and sickly child we had brought back from Boston.

'Are we doing the right thing for her?' Mark asked. I looked at her happy smiling face on the TV screen and thought of the frightened nine-year-old girl who lay in the room above me, too ill to move, and I couldn't be certain.

'We have to remember our daughter is a little fighter. That's what makes her unique. We have to hope that she will get through this and be stronger and live longer,' Mark said.

The next day Hayley seemed a bit perkier, it seemed that the anti-sickness drugs had taken effect and by day three she was back to her old self and we could breathe a sigh of relief.

We began monthly appointments with Dr Whincup who was monitoring Hayley's progress and reporting back to the doctors in Boston in between visits. For the first month her weight actually dipped due to the early bouts of sickness and diarrhoea. But once that was under control, and her appetite was back to normal, she started to pick up and we noticed her weight crept up month by month. Several months into the trial, Dr Whincup noticed that her blood pressure was creeping up to a rate that was above normal for a young child. Hayley was put on a 24-hour blood pressure monitor which meant that she had to wear a tight cuff on her arm day and night to measure her blood pressure when she was awake and sleeping. After that, Dr Whincup prescribed the beta-blocker Atenanol to bring her blood pressure down and reduce the risk of heart disease or a stroke. This new drug brought additional worries. The side-effects were fainting and dizziness and I was concerned that she might suffer from dizzy spells or sickness at school. In order to eliminate any problems we gave her the tablets when she came home from school and we could watch out for any problems.

For the rest of the year, and throughout 2008, we continued our trips to Boston for the drug trial. Every 16 weeks Hayley would get another dose of FTIs and she would be measured and have her body tested. On our first return visit there was not much to see. The doctors didn't give too much away, but they seemed pleased with the way it was progressing. The side-effects that had scared us so much in the early days had receded and she was improving. In between each visit we would notice something new in Hayley's development. She had grown a couple of centimetres. Her eyebrows had started to grow and she had a layer of light downy hair on her arms. It gave us the glimmer of hope that we needed to help us to carry on.

Filming one of my documentaries on the beach at Bexhill, 2004

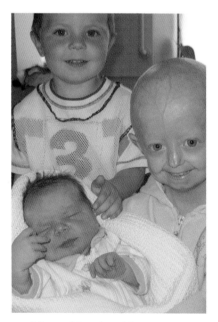

Me and Louis with our new
baby sister Ruby, 2005

Me and Mum on holiday
in Egypt, 2006

Me and Dad with a snake on
holiday in Egypt, 2006

Me and Dad wrestle alligators on
holiday in Florida, 2003

Mum and Dad's wedding day, July 2006

A bridesmaid at Mum and Dad's
wedding, July 2006

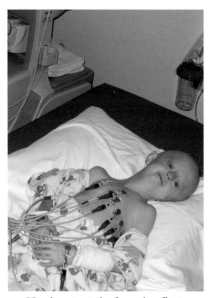

Having tests before the first
progeria drug trial in
America, 2007

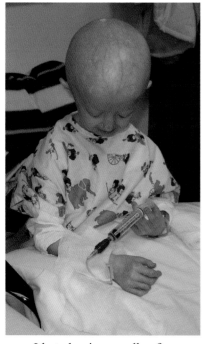

I hate having needles for
blood tests, 2008

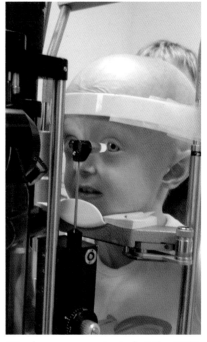

Having my eyes tested at the NIH
trials, 2005

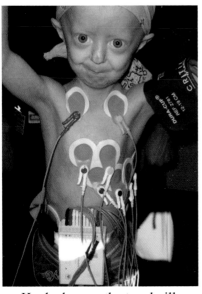

Hooked up on the treadmill, 2005

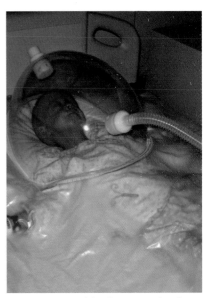

More tests, this time monitoring how many calories I burn when I lie down, 2007

Our family with Dr Leslie Gordon and Scott Berns of the Progeria Research Foundation and their son Sam in Boston, 2008

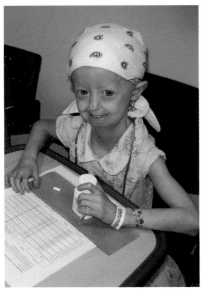

Making history as the first child in Europe to try the FTI drug, 2007

Me and Michiel presented with awards for completing the triple drug trial, pictured with Amber and Louis, 2009

Me and Michiel in my hot tub, 2007

My first day at Bexhill High
School, 2009

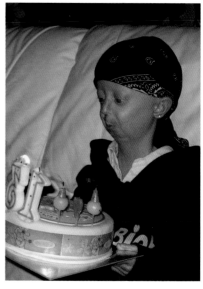

My 13th birthday, 2010

Posing with my friends at a sleep over, 2010

With my 'little brother and sister' Ruby and Louis, August 2011

Watching my book in production, 2011
photo courtesy Channel 5/Rabbit Productions

Preparing for the photoshoot for my book cover, July 2011
photo courtesy Channel 5/Rabbit Productions

Me and my best friend Erin, 2011

Chapter 23
Hayley
Hope Is when Mum Stops Crying

WHEN WE GOT TO BOSTON we met with Michiel and his family and it was like being on holiday, so I wasn't too worried. We had left Ruby at home with a family friend so it was just me, Mum, Dad, and Louis who went. In Boston we all went on the trolley bus with Michiel and his mum and dad and sister, Amber. We stopped at the aquarium and saw giant sharks and sting rays, which were really cool.

But after a couple of days we had to go to the hospital and they started doing lots of tests again.

When we got there the nurses weighed and measured me and did an ECG on my heart. Then they wanted to do a skin biopsy which is like scraping off a bit of the skin from my arm. They also wanted to take one from Mum and Dad. First they put a numbing cream on my arm and I had to wait for one hour. When the cream made my arm numb the nurse got out a needle. But when the nurse got closer with the needle I said I didn't want to do it. The needle was like a corkscrew and they wanted to put it in under my arm and take out the skin. When someone said I would only need one stitch, I thought, no way. The nurses gave me a lolly but I still wouldn't do it. I felt really bad after because I made Mum and Dad wait an hour for nothing. Mum tried to bribe me with sweets and said she would even buy me a new phone. It almost worked but I started to cry and she said 'Fine you don't have to do it.' But I think she was peed off. Afterwards I wished I had done it

On the day I got to take the tablet everyone was making a big deal about it. I had to go in a room with Mum, Dad, and the doctors. I felt a little bit scared but I kept telling myself, 'You're gonna get hair. You're gonna grow tall.' First I had to swallow a Tic Tac to show them I could swallow it. At first I was afraid it would get stuck in my throat and make me choke. Then they gave me the real tablet and I put it on my tongue took a big mouthful of water. Mum looked scared. I think she thought I was going to choke or something. But I gulped it down easily. Then I poked my tongue out to show it was gone. Everyone in the room went 'yay!' and they were all taking pictures. It was scary but really exciting at the same time.

When we got home I felt really sick. When I told Mum and Dad they were worried and that made me scared. It was really horrible. I felt sick, and then I felt tired so I slept. Because I was sleeping I didn't eat much and that made me feel sick again. It kept going round for ages and I thought, why am I doing this if it makes me feel worse? Dad went out and got some more tablets. After I started taking them I felt better and Mum and Dad stopped worrying. Mum tried to make me feel better by saying that if I jumped up and down they could hear me rattle because I was so full of pills.

I started having the tablets twice a day – one in the morning before school and one at tea-time. To see if the tablets were doing any good and making me grow Mum made a height chart on the kitchen door and some days I would stand and measure myself against it. I remember once being 3cm taller and I was really pleased. I thought it must be working. Mum and Dad started taking me to see Dr Whincup more often and he was pleased with the way I was growing too. I started to feel like I was getting stronger. I could run about in school and do star jumps with my friends. But before the drugs I was too weak to jump very much at all.

Sometimes, when Mum and Dad weren't looking, I would look in the mirror to see if I had more hair, and I did. I started to grow eyebrows like the other kids in school, and some hair. I said to myself, 'You're turning into a monkey.' Mum used to tease me that I was growing a moustache like Dad, but she was only joking. I hope I don't get a moustache, but lately I have noticed some more hairs on my arms and my chin. I think I might be getting a beard. I hope I don't grow a moustache and beard because I would have to start shaving and that would be embarrassing.

When I started the trials my biggest dream was to have long hair that I could tie back in a pink hair band. Every time we go back to Boston the doctors check if my hair has grown. They draw a little square on the back of my head and count the hairs in it. The first time there were no hairs and now there are seven hairs. I say 'Wow! Seven hairs!' I know that's not a lot, but it is to me.

The drug hasn't worked out quite like I had wished. When I realised I wasn't going to get long hair, I was quite sad. But now it's OK. Just the other day I looked in the mirror and I found a few more little black eyebrows. They are really tiny, you can barely see them, but it's good I have some. I don't want to get really thick eyebrows. I would like to grow more hair and get taller. If I get eyelashes I can put mascara on them. Since I've been taking the drugs I do feel taller.

I am definitely getting taller. At first I noticed it when I stood up in the bath. It used to be that I couldn't see myself in the mirror unless I stood on a bowl. I know I am definitely taller because when I open the fridge I bang my head. It used to just skim my head but now I have to duck when I open it. I know now that the drugs won't ever make me completely better, and I won't look like a normal person, but it still makes me feel really happy that they are working.

One day when I was eleven and I was bored with nothing else to do, I sat down in my bedroom and thought about the drugs. Usually I try not to think about it too often, it's not something that's always on my mind, but this day I remember thinking how cool it was and I was glad I had decided to do it. I thought progeria was so weird but it's kind of cool because I have to go to Boston and I don't have to do much work. I don't know any people who have been away from England, yet I get to go on cool holidays all the time.

It's like the drugs are making my mum stronger too. She used to be so sad and sometimes she used to cry when she was talking about me to her friends and Nanna. But now I have been taking the tablets she has stopped crying, and that's good. I think she knows there's hope.

Chapter 24
Kerry
High School Days

WE HAD ALWAYS LIVED one year at a time and never daring to plan ahead when it came to Hayley's education. When she was younger I had thought that there was no point in wasting six hours a day in school, learning things that she might never get to use, when she could be travelling the world and trying new experiences. But the older she became I realised going to high school was a normal progression. In July 2009 it was time for Hayley to leave the comfortable surroundings of her primary school, where all the teachers and pupils knew and cared for her, and prepare to make the step to secondary education.

The obvious choice of big school was Bexhill High School, where most of the children from her class would be going. However, Mark and I worried that Hayley might find it a bit of a culture shock. She was moving from a small class of 20 children in her primary school to a school of 1500 pupils. With so many older children from a wider area, I worried that Hayley might become more of a target for bullies. Up until that point she had lived her life relatively protected by her class teachers and her close friends. Mark and I started looking at other schools and considering whether our finances could stretch to the thousands of pounds it would cost to send her to a private girls' school, where we imagined she would have more protection from playground bullies. Hayley was determined she wanted to follow her friends to Bexhill High School, so we dropped the costly idea of private education. She didn't seem to be worried about being in a school with bigger children whom she didn't know.

In the final days of her primary school, Hayley's teacher took her and her best friends Erin and Lydia for a tour of Bexhill High. When Hayley came home she was buzzing. 'Teacher says I can dissect a frog at Bexhill High,' she announced. It made me laugh knowing how much she disliked having needles yet she was not at all squeamish about cutting up a dead frog. She told me how during the tour of the school the headmistress had showed the girls around the biology laboratory where her friends dared her to stroke a snake. They were also given the opportunity to ask their new teachers about anything that might be worrying them.

'Erin told the teacher she had eczema and asked whether it would matter that she had to wear her jumper when it was warm. And the teacher told her that her parents could sign a form so that they would know and it would be all right,' Hayley said. 'Then Lydia asked if she would get bullied because she was short.'

'What did the teacher say?' I fished, hoping to get an insight into Hayley's own bullying fears.

'She said bullying wasn't an issue at Bexhill High.' I had already spoken with Hayley's teachers and been told there was a strong anti-bullying policy in place and they came down hard on any pupils they identified as bullies.

Unlike the start of primary school, shopping for uniform wasn't an issue. The school was very helpful in getting a navy skirt and jumper made in Hayley's size and a shorter clip-on school tie which was easier for her to wear. They even arranged a special bandana with the school badge on the front, which she wore for a few weeks before deciding she stood out too much and reverted to her own navy bandana.

The morning of her first day at Bexhill High arrived and, once again, I had more butterflies than Hayley. She packed her pencil case, notebook, geometry set and her dinner money into her new backpack and waited for the school taxi.

As we walked up to the school gates she dropped my hand and started edging ahead. She looked so tiny and fragile compared to all of the other children. I was suddenly overwhelmed by my maternal instinct to wrap her up in cotton wool.

'Do you want me to carry your back pack?' I asked.

'Mum, I can do it,' she said.

'But there are other mothers doing it,' I protested.

'Mum, I can do it,' she said again and marched off to join her best friends, Erin and Lydia, in the playground, leaving me out on the pavement with the other mums.

At the end of the day I was back at the gates waiting to meet her. The school had allowed her to leave earlier than the other children to avoid getting caught in the mad scrum for the doors when the bell rang at home-time. It was the one concession where Hayley didn't mind being treated differently. Elsewhere in the school she wanted to be the same as the other children. Originally, the school had allocated her a lower desk and special chairs, but she hated being singled out for special treatment. When they moved to a brand new school building which had been built with lower desks in all of the classrooms she was much happier. Each classroom pod had a selection of different types of chairs including six lower padded stools which she was able to sit on with the other pupils. She would not use anything that singled her out as being different from the other kids.

Throughout her high school life, Mark and I have always insisted that Hayley shouldn't be given any special treatment and this proved to be the case one day when I had a call, to say that Hayley was being kept behind after class for being naughty. It turned out that she had drawn on the shirt of one of the boys in her class and was rightly being punished for it. The boy's mother called me afterwards to apologise saying that she had asked the school not to reprimand Hayley. But I say, 'You do the crime, you do the time,' and Hayley had to learn that her progeria didn't protect her from punishment. It was her first, and I hope last, taste of detention.

In general, the teachers at the school have been very supportive of Hayley and her progeria throughout her school life. They have held special events and cake bakes to raise awareness and money for Hayley's charity. While Hayley is in school she has a teaching assistant shadowing her at a safe distance during break times to make sure she doesn't get knocked over. And whenever she is not feeling well the school will call me and let me know. I always tell them I would rather they call for nothing than risk leaving it. My biggest fear is that when her time comes I am not going to be there, so I don't mind being called for a false alarm.

Just before 4 p.m. on February 17 2011 the alarm bells rang in my head when I got a phone call from Hayley's school. I was in the house on my own as Mark had just taken the car to pick Ruby and Louis up from school. 'Nothing to worry about,' the voice on the other end said. My heart thumped. 'Hayley has fallen over and we think she's hurt her leg.'

'Has she bruised it?' I asked. This was a regular problem with Hayley's fragile skin. She was always covered in bruises from bumping her head on the fridge door or brushing her arm against her bedroom door and quite often the bruises looked worse than they actually were.

'We don't know,' the school replied.

'Is she crying?' I asked. Again, they didn't know as the caller wasn't in the same room.

'Wait there, we'll be up straight away.' I put down the phone and called Mark. Five minutes later we were ushered into the school gym where Hayley was lying on a big blue crash mat. She looked a bit washed-out but she was trying to put on a brave face and was laughing and giggling while sitting on the mat surrounded by her friends.

'What have you done?' I asked.

'I've fallen over, but I don't want an ambulance,' she insisted.

I offered to carry her to the car but as I tried to pick her up, she yelled out in pain. I couldn't move her, and that's when it hit me that this was more serious than another bump. The teachers cleared the area and called an ambulance which was able to park right outside the entrance to avoid any on-lookers. It was hard to be standing by and not able to do anything as she screamed when the ambulance man lifted her onto the stretcher. That's when I noticed that one leg was three inches shorter than the other and panicked that she had done some serious damage.

At the hospital, the doctors X-rayed Hayley's leg and discovered she had dislocated her hip. She was taken down to the operating theatre and her hip was put back into place. It was an anxious time for Mark and me as it was the first time she had ever had a general anaesthetic. It was crucial that the doctors got the dose right. The dose for an average 13-year-old would be too much for her, but doctors were afraid that a dose that was equivalent to her weight might not be enough to knock her out. While we waited Hayley became more and more anxious. 'What if I don't wake up, Mummy?' she cried.

'Of course you will. And when you come round we'll get you the iPad you've always wanted,' I joked, trying to keep her mind off what lay ahead. When the mask was put over her face, she froze. She counted backwards from 10, and soon she was out. As they wheeled her into the theatre I stood in the doorway, not wanting to close the door on her, until a nurse came and led me away.

Chapter 25
Hayley
Why I Hate School

IT WAS WEIRD STARTING my new school because everyone seemed really big and I was really tiny.

In the primary school there were kids who were littler than me but at Bexhill High I was, and still am, the smallest. At first I was afraid that someone might knock me over.

When I had to choose my big school Mum said 'Wouldn't you like to go to an all-girls school?' I told her I wanted to be with my friends. I asked Erin and Lydia what school they were going to go to. When they said they were going to Bexhill High I told Mum that that was where I wanted to go. I told her, 'I want to be with my friends, thank you very much.'

Our teacher at the primary school took us to Bexhill High to have a look and ask questions. They showed us the biology class. Dad said to me that you have to cut up frogs in big school. I was too shy to ask the teacher but Lydia said, 'Hayley wants to know if she can dissect a frog?' The teacher said we would. I thought that big school would be cool.

On my first day at big school all the year sevens had to go into the hall for assembly. There were so many other kids there I was scared I might get lost or lose my friends. I sat down near the front of the hall with my friends. Then we had to stand up when the headmaster came in.

'Good morning year seven,' he said.

'Good morning, sir,' we said. He started talking, telling us something about beginning a journey that helps to prepare us to make our choices for the future.

Then he said there was to be absolutely no violence in school, like fighting and pushing and shoving to get to the front of queues.

'That is totally unacceptable,' he said and asked us if we understood.

We all nodded. I felt happier. I was scared that I might get knocked over.

In my class's form room I had a special chair and desk which was higher than the others. I had two other chairs that I was supposed to carry around to lessons because I was too little to sit on the normal chairs. But I didn't like them. In biology my special desk was near the front next to the teacher, but I didn't like sitting there and being treated differently. So I asked the teacher if I could move and she let me move further back to sit next to Erin.

In school they gave me a special chair to reach the desks but my mum said I didn't have to use it if I didn't want to. In class we have blue and yellow chairs which are really hard and we have cushion chairs called pouffes. I like to sit on the pouffes.

The playground in my school is ginormous, not like my old school. Everywhere is really busy and I am afraid I will get knocked over. When I have to walk past boys playing football, Erin and Lydia walk in front of me to protect me from getting knocked over by the ball. During the break times I like to go to the library where it's quiet and safe. I don't like going outside as there's nothing to do except stand around, and it's noisy with everyone shouting. No one shouts in the library. It's not allowed.

I am lucky that I have amazing friends. I have become more self-conscious as I get older but I don't think anyone would say anything bad behind my back. Obviously people who don't know me probably would and some people have, but I ignore it.

I know I have loads of friends at school who will stick up for me. If someone is staring at me they say, 'Stop staring! Leave her alone.' They are not afraid to stick up for me even if the kid doing the staring is bigger than them. Erin will stick up for me even if the other kids are much bigger than her. She is fearless. I am really lucky to have good friends like them. Sometimes when we are in the playground my friends get down on their knees to talk to me, but this annoys me. I say, 'You can stand up, you know. I can hear you.'

I like doing cooking in school. I made cheese straws, cheesecake and flapjacks like Nanna makes. I cooked risotto as well. I had never had it before and now it's one of my favourite meals. It's easy to make, but it takes for ever. Mum and I make it with carrots, onions, garlic peppers and stock. I would eat it every day if I could. Mum says I don't eat a lot but that's because I always feel full. I think it must be because of my progeria because Erin can eat loads more than me.

Once I had detention because I drew on a boy called Kyle's shirt because he was annoying me. The teacher caught me and I had to stay in class late and Mum had to pick me up after the other kids had all gone home. It was annoying because Kyle's mum wasn't mad about it. But Mum said it was right that I should get detention because I am no different to the other kids and that's what I get for being naughty. The next day Kyle said 'What kind of smiley face was that?' He wasn't bothered I had drawn on him.

Now I am 13, I hate school. The work is pointless. I like reading books at home, but not in school because they have rubbish books at school. When we have to go and choose a book to read I always get there last and all they have left is a dictionary. I have to read a dictionary for half an hour which is boring. So when we are supposed to be reading, Erin and I talk behind our books.

I hate my teachers too. They split me and Erin up for no reason. We were just sitting there talking and the teacher made Erin sit on another table. The best thing about school is the lunch time and home time.

I was pleased when I first dislocated my hip last February because it meant I didn't have to go to school. Mum arranged for me to have lessons on the computer at home.

It all happened when I was in the PE hall watching my friend trampolining. While she was waiting to go on I was sitting on a bench, and I stood up to get my bag from the other side of the room and I just sort of tripped over the bench and my left hip popped out. It really hurt, but I didn't cry. At first I was going, 'Owww,' and shouting. Miss Baker, the teacher, was really nice to me. She told two of my friends Fred and Charlie to get a crash mat. Everyone was gathering around, so Miss Baker told them all to go away. There was just me, Fred and Charlie. The teachers at the school asked me if I wanted an ambulance and I said no because I didn't know I had dislocated my hip. Then they said, 'Let's call your mum.' While we were waiting for Mum the teachers tried to get me to stand up and that's when it really hurt and I said, 'Ow!'

Mum, Dad, Louis and Ruby rushed in. By this time it

was nearly home-time so Fred and Charlie had gone home. When Mum tried to pick me up she couldn't do it because it really hurt. She said, 'Call an ambulance.' I was just thinking, here we go, because I didn't think there was much wrong with my leg. I just thought I had fallen and badly bruised it.

When we got to hospital I had an X-ray and they said it was dislocated. I was thinking, what are they going to do with me? When they said they were going to put me under general anaesthetic I was really scared. I thought, what if I don't wake up? They put the mask on and told me to count down from 10 to 1. They said, 'You probably won't get to 7.' I was holding my mum's hand and started counting. I said 'I love you, Mum,' and then I was gone. I remember it was 12.20 a.m. when I went into the operation and 1.20 a.m. when I woke up. I know that because there was a clock on the wall. At first I felt sick and I wanted to gag where there had been a tube stuffed down my throat. I was really tired as well. Then I saw my mum and said, 'Am I going to get an iPad?' That's all I cared about because when we were waiting in the hospital Mum said she would buy me one. The next day I was allowed to go home with my mum.

I didn't have to go to school for a couple of weeks. But the next day my friend Erin came round after school and said there were some kids who said that I had died. That was really annoying. I thought that it was so typical of the kids in school. Why don't they just get their facts right? Just because I fell and had to have an ambulance doesn't mean I've died. I told Erin to tell them I had dislocated my hip and I was fine, thank you very much.

I can't wait to leave school. I know what I want to be. I want to be a DJ or a film maker like James and Nicki who have made programmes about me. Sometimes when they are filming me they leave their camera in our house and when they are not looking I pretend to be a film maker. When I am a famous director I want to make chick flicks like my favourite movie *Confessions of a Teenage Drama Queen*, which is about a girl who moves away from New York and has to make new friends in a different place, but she gets into lots of trouble.

I am always listening to Radio 1 so I think it would be cool to get a job as a DJ. I could play lots of different kinds of music and talk in between tracks. We have a radio station in school and they let me go on and talk about the fund-raising we were doing for the Progeria Reunion. I got to play a record for my mum so I chose *Next to You* by Justin Bieber and Chris Brown because that was one of her favourites. I think I would make a good DJ. Maybe one day I will write to Fearne Cotton who is my favourite DJ on Radio 1 and ask her if she needs some help.

If I can't be a film maker or a DJ I want to be a beautician. This year I had to choose my options and I have chosen hair and beauty. Me and Erin want to run our own beauty salon. Erin says we should call it Magic Fingers but I don't like that name, I think Stars is better. Sometimes we dream about what our salon will be like. It will have a red carpet and a mud bath in the middle and it will be somewhere that isn't Bexhill. I can't wait until I am old enough to leave school.

Chapter 26
Kerry
Tough Choices

BY SPRING 2009 AS the first drug trials in Boston were coming to an end we received news from the Progeria Research Foundation of another trial which doctors hoped would have even better results by using a combination of different drugs. The research team had identified two extra drugs that combined with the FTI drug Hayley was currently taking could prove even more effective. The additional drugs were statins, usually given to patients with high cholesterol, and a bisphosphonate drug used to help osteoporosis sufferers.

There was just one fly in the ointment. At that point we had not had any official results from the first trial and once again we were in a dilemma as to whether or not to expose Hayley to another cocktail of drugs. Our gut feeling was that it was working. Before she started taking the FTIs she was growing an average of 2cm every six months, but her growth rate had almost doubled since the trial started. Dr Whincup also seemed to be pleased with her progress during our monthly check-ups at the Conquest Hospital.

In Boston the research team had started conducting a month-long mini-trial of the triple drug on five children aged between two and three to check if they were able to tolerate the potential side-effects. When the results of these trials proved satisfactory they would move on to a larger group, giving us the opportunity to include Hayley.

I read out the detail of my email from Dr Gordon at the foundation to Mark. 'It says that bisphosphonates are used to help elderly people with their bones. The drug is administered intravenously and its common side-effects are fatigue, anaemia, muscle aches, fever and swelling in the legs.'

'Do we really want to put her through another round of needles and possible side-effects for something that will make her grow just a little bit?' Mark asked. I shared his concern. If we wanted to take part this drug wasn't simply a question of popping a pill, it would mean Hayley would have to be hooked up to a drip for 30 minutes at a time. She hated needles and I wasn't sure we could force her to have more injections. Once again we were torn. Mark and I wanted to give Hayley every possible chance of prolonging her life, but not at any cost.

To help us learn more we visited a progeria expert at Brunel University in the UK. Dr Ian Kill and his team of scientists were studying the effects of ageing in progeria children and normal adults. In his laboratory Dr Kill was working on fruit flies, which apparently have a similar genetic make-up to humans, to find ways of slowing down this ageing. Through a microscope we were shown the flies they had injected with progeria cells. They were not buzzing around like normal flies, but they were crawling around half dead. Dr Kill then sat us down and explained how the FTI drugs, which Hayley had been taking for two years, were able to block the pathway of the progeria cells in the body. But he told us that sometimes this happened late in the process and that's why his team of scientists were trying to find ways of starting the blocking earlier.

They had discovered that the pathway of ageing was similar to the one used in the production of cholesterol. He showed Mark and I a diagram with arrows pointing to lots of long names. It meant nothing to us, but the long and short of what he was telling us was that statins, which are taken by people with high cholesterol, could be used to treat progeria. By a fortunate coincidence, Hayley was already taking statins, prescribed by Dr Whincup. He had first prescribed them because both my mum and I suffered from high blood pressure. Armed with this new information, Mark and I decided it was worth a try.

Before leaving for Boston that August for the final session of the original FTI trials and the start of the triple drug trial we had another consultation with Dr Whincup for the results of Hayley's ultra-sound kidney scan. One of the known side-effects of taking bisphosphonate was that it could cause calcium to build up in the body. Previously there had been some concern that Hayley might be showing a build-up of calcium on her kidneys and the Boston doctors needed proof that Hayley's kidneys were fit and functioning well. The results showed no deterioration in her kidneys, liver or heart. 'No lumps, no nasty things. You're good to go,' Dr Whincup said to Hayley as he gave his blessing for the new round of drugs.

During our visit to Boston, Hayley and her Belgian friend Michiel were presented with trophies for completing the first-ever progeria clinical drug trial. They were among 45 children from 24 different countries who would be taking part in the new study. The group also included some progeria children who had been too young to take part in the original trial and others who were just starting the single FTI drug trial. The Boston Children's Hospital and its partner the Dana-Farber Cancer Institute had received a $3.1 million grant to fund the cost of the trials. By signing up we were committing to another two years of trips to Boston.

After the usual rounds of blood tests and tissue samples, Hayley was hooked up to the machine which delivered the bisphosphonate into her blood. She had to lie still on a bed while the drug was pumped into her blood stream through a canula in the back of her hand. It was a boring process and one that would have to be repeated every six months but Hayley was already beginning to treat the Boston Children's Hospital as her second home and was happy to lie there playing on her Nintendo DS game while the drugs did their work. When her 30 minutes were up everyone gave her the thumbs-up which seemed to be a good sign. Sometimes that was the only way we could tell if things were going well, we watched the doctor's expressions. If they smiled we knew they were happy and we could take some comfort from them too. The doctors explained that if the three drugs worked effectively then the progerin would become 'paralyzed' and Hayley's progeria could be improved. The scientists working for the Progeria Research Foundation say they are learning a lot about ageing from Hayley and the other progeria children, particularly when it comes to heart disease. Children with progeria don't smoke and don't have high cholesterol so scientists are able to study the effects progerin has on heart disease.

'Our initial reasons for coming to Boston were purely selfish to give Hayley a chance of longer life,' I reflected to Mark on our journey home. 'Yet it's mind-blowing to think that these drugs we are giving her could help millions of older people around the world who suffer from heart disease. Not only are we saving Hayley's life, Hayley could be saving the lives of others.'

*   *   *

For the next two years we continued visiting Boston for the triple drug trial treatment.

Unlike the first trial there were no bad side-effects and we felt that the trips were worth it. Hayley continued to grow and her check-ups with Dr Whincup continued to bear positive results. A CT scan of her heart during this time showed none of the deterioration in her arteries which he had expected. In real terms Hayley's body was then equivalent to people in their nineties. We knew that the biggest killer of progeria children was heart disease so confirmation that her heart was still strong was good news. But the greatest boost to our confidence came when Hayley visited another specialist team who had not seen her for more than a year. They were surprised by how healthy she looked. They said her they could see an improvement in her face, her cheeks were fuller and her skin was healthier. Being with her every day we noticed changes for the better but often wondered if it was more wishful thinking on our part; to have our thoughts endorsed by a professional was a real boost to our optimism.

My other great fear for Hayley as she got older was mobility. Over the years at the Progeria Reunions we had met several children who were handicapped by their prematurely ageing bodies. Like some elderly people they had to rely on wheelchairs to get around because they were too frail to walk on their own. After Hayley's accident in the school gym I began to worry that her bones were beginning to let her down. Hayley was so full of life I knew it would kill her to lose the use of her legs.

A few weeks after her accident in school we had a second scare when she slipped on a washing powder capsule in the kitchen and dislocated her left hip again. It was such a silly, typically childish accident. She was trying

159

to burst the plastic washing powder bubble with her foot and slipped. Seeing her in such agony upset me. I worried that this was the start of a major problem. I called the ambulance and again she was rushed into the Conquest Hospital for an operation to put the leg back in its socket.

We found ourselves back in the accident and emergency department a few weeks later again. It was beginning to feel like groundhog day. There was obviously a weakness in her hip by now as she had just turned around on her bed and her leg had popped out of its socket again.

'We think Hayley would benefit from a leg brace. She will need to wear it 24 hours a day for six months to give her muscles and ligaments the chance to repair themselves,' the doctor advised me.

'Wouldn't a hip replacement be better?' I asked, knowing that there was no way on earth I could persuade Hayley to wear the uncomfortable and ugly leg brace for half a year. But the doctor explained that there was no guarantee a hip replacement operation would work in Hayley's case.

Not happy with the suggestions we sought a second opinion with a specialist in London, who did a CAT scan of Hayley's hips. The scan showed that whereas most normal people have C-shaped hip sockets which securely cup the ball joint on the top of the thigh, Hayley's was so worn down it was virtually flat. So even if they did operate to replace the hip joint there was no guarantee the artificial socket would be secure. The conclusion was that the brace was the only alternative.

Hayley was unhappy with the idea and I had my work cut out convincing her otherwise. Then a few weeks later she dislocated both her left and right hips while she was walking up a flight of stairs and the decision was made for us and the hospital ordered Hayley a leg brace. When it arrived she wasn't at all happy and I can't say that I blamed her. It was such an ugly, uncomfortable contraption, it swallowed her up.

During her periods of convalescence I was worried that she would be falling behind with her school work. But Hayley's teachers were great and quickly made arrangements for her to take her lessons online. Every day we sat down together and Hayley would learn maths, English or science and when she was done she would sit quietly in her bedroom and read. It was the ideal solution. Hayley was happier not having to go into school and I felt safer knowing that she was back under my protection.

Chapter 27
Hayley
Just Call Me Robo-Chick

EVERYONE TELLS ME I'M brave. And when I go to hospital I try to be brave. But when I'm not in hospital I'm a big wimp. I'm even scared of spiders and the dark.

When Mum told me about the new drug trial, that had to be injected, I wasn't very keen on the idea. I don't like having needles but I thought, if it will make me better, then I have to do it I suppose. I asked if they had tablets I could take instead of having an injection but they didn't. The injection was a bit scary, I was worried in case anything went wrong. First I had to have a little needle stuck in my arm and taped over, then they put another needle with the drugs into it. The needle hurt when it went in the first time and I felt a bit sick. I had a tube coming out of my arm which went to a machine with numbers on it. I couldn't really feel the bisphosphonate going into my body. It was going so slow, it made a snail look like a cheetah. I had to lie there and do nothing for ages. Then I had to take some medicine because they said I might have headaches, or achey bones and stuff, but all the time I have been taking the drugs nothing has been wrong. I take them to make sure. If they say it will make me better I might as well take it, that's what I think.

When I dislocated my hip the first time, Mum said I

was really brave because it hurt so much. It hurt even more when I did it the second time but I wasn't so scared because I knew what to expect. It happened again when I was in the kitchen with Mum. I asked if I could jump on a washing machine tablet to burst it. I stomped on it and it didn't pop so I started jumping on it with both of my feet and I twisted wrong and my hip popped out again. My mum called an ambulance. I just thought, here we go again, while mum was crying. I was in so much pain it was horrible.

The third time it happened I was having a sleep-over with Erin and my cousin Sophie. Me and Sophie were lying on the bed and Erin was on mattress on the floor. I was doing Sophie's make-up but I couldn't see very well because it was a bit dark. So I went to open the curtains and I twisted on the duvet and I felt my leg pop out. We had to cancel the sleep-over and I had to go to hospital again, which was bad.

After that the doctors said I should wear a brace. I said, 'No way!' It was a big ugly metal thing that they said I would have to wear for six months. It looked really uncomfortable and I didn't want to have it. Mum said that maybe there was an operation I could have but I would have to stay in intensive care for a week and stay in hospital for a while. Then I would have to stay in bed, but I didn't want to do that either. Anyway the doctors put my leg back in and I went home.

I was happy when Mum said I didn't have to go to school because of my hips, so I could do my work on the computer instead. I had to do maths, English, science and citizenship and it was much better than having to go to school. After school Erin would come round to my house and we'd catch up on all the gossip so I didn't feel like I was missing anything. Whenever Erin comes to my house she likes watching the Disney Channel because she says her mum can't afford it at their house. We watch Hannah Montana and sometimes we watch the Music Channel but not much. Other kids in school like the Music Channel but I think music videos are boring – unless they are by Justin Bieber. I like cartoons better, they make me laugh.

The last time I dislocated my hip I was walking up stairs with my dad. I was three steps from the top when I caught my toe and twisted funny. I didn't even fall because Dad caught me but I felt both my left hip and my right one pop out. I could tell that Dad was scared because he had never seen me do it before. He tried to lift me up but he couldn't hold me under my bum like he usually did because it hurt too much. So I had to put my arms around his shoulders and hold on tight and he held my body and carried me into the bedroom. I said to him 'I think I've done the other one.' I started to cry because I was so uncomfortable. When I hurt my left hip I could lie on my right one so I could ease the pressure. But I couldn't lie on either side because it hurt so much. So I had to lie on my back. I was crying. Louis and Ruby were crying too because they were scared for me. They were both really helpful. Ruby watched out for the ambulance and Louis was rubbing my head and my hand while we waited for the ambulance.

When we got to the hospital I had gas and air again. I love that stuff. It doesn't smell or taste of anything but when you breathe in it makes you feel like you're away with the fairies. I took three puffs and I started giggling. Just before I went under the nurse was holding my hand. Dad took Ruby home to fetch my pyjamas and Mum and Louis stayed by my bed. Louis was so sweet as I was going down to the operating theatre he was holding my hand and rubbing my head and it made me cry.

After I came around from the operation Louis was really scared for me. I said, 'Don't worry, it won't happen again.'

That's when the doctors said I had to wear the dreaded leg brace. It's horrible. It has a big thick metal belt that goes around my waist and metal rods that are strapped around my legs. Mum calls me 'Robo-Chick' because I look like a robot when I am wearing it. The only good thing I can say about it is that it is purple and that's my favourite colour. The first time I only wore it for four hours and then I took it off and said, 'I can't wear that.' It was too uncomfortable. I am supposed to wear it for six months, 24/7. The only time I take it off is when I have a bath or shower and I'm not even supposed to do that. It's really annoying. I thought it might be a bit comfortable because it had purple padding around it, but it's not. When I sit in the car I can't even lean back because it sticks in me and hurts. When I am lying in bed it feels horrible and I can't move. If I want to go to the toilet in the night I have to wake Louis up and ask him to take it off for me, because I'm not supposed to. In the beginning I used to wrap my cardigan around it to hide it when I went out because it looked so bad. I'm stuck with it until my hips get better. I suppose it's better than being in a wheelchair or intensive care or something. I'm getting used to it now, I don't care so much. I've found that I can tuck my iPhone into it so it has its uses after all. But I am counting down the days until the time I can take it off for good and my legs will be better.

Chapter 28
Kerry
Pressures of Progeria

THEY SAY THAT DIVORCE, debt and moving house are the most stressful things in life, but I bet the people who said it have never tried to organise a holiday for progeria families. When the Sunshine Foundation charity, which had organised the American reunions for the previous 27 years, announced it had to cancel the 2010 reunion due to the worldwide recession, the drop in the number of charity donations and the spiralling costs of making it happen, Mark and I decided to step in.

'The reunions have been a lifeline for so many families like us. It would be such a shame for the children if they stop for ever,' Mark said when we first heard the news. So in a moment of what I can only now call utter madness, I said, 'Let's organise our own.' For years we had said how great it would be to organise a reunion in England, now we were putting our talk into action.

Working closely with our friends at the Progeria Family Circle, who held annual conferences for all the families in Europe, we arranged a date and place – August 6 to 12 2010 in Ashford, Kent. The location was close to our home but also close to the ports and airports for the families travelling across the English Channel. As word spread of our plans 16 families signed up for the holiday. There was just one problem, we didn't have a venue or any money to pay for it.

'We're going to have to pull our fingers out and get moving if we're going to have a reunion in August,' I said to Mark one day in February. 'We've only got six months. We don't want to let everyone down for a second time.'

First I had to find a venue. I rang one hotel which looked out over the beach in Hythe.

'I've got a budget of £17,500 and I need 32 rooms with breakfast included for six nights from August 6 to 12,' I bluffed. Actually we had only £700 in our reunion fund. The person on the other end of the phone went off and came back 10 minutes later saying they could do it for £14,500. It was under budget but still £13,800 more than we could afford. With that figure in mind I rang around a couple of hotels to see if I could get a better deal. The events manager at the Ashford International Hotel came up trumps. For the same price they would match my other quotes and throw in lots of extras including the farewell party on our last night. Plus they had a swimming pool. It was a deal. Mark and I had just 161 days to raise what was the equivalent of almost a year's wages. No pressure!

Cap in hand, I went to every well-known charity I could think of. The National Lottery's Good Causes, Comic Relief, Children in Need, you name it, I tried it. But it seemed that with every application I made, I faced rejection. It wasn't a community event. We didn't have criminal record checks on all the people we were inviting. Most of the children were not based in the UK. The list went on and with every 'no' I received I became more depressed. The Progeria Family Circle had agreed to pay for the hotel accommodation for the visitors but Mark and I still had to come up with the cost of the flights, day trips and food, We still needed to find thousands of pounds in cash and goodwill to make it a week to remember. With a couple of months to go we checked our measly total. 'We're going to have to cancel,' Mark said.

'No way. We can't let the children down. We'll have to take out a bank loan,' I replied, kicking off what turned into an almighty row. Our relationship in recent years had been rocky to put it mildly, but the pressure of organising the reunion was pushing us to the limits. We seemed to be fighting over anything and everything.

Then in June – less than two months before the reunion – Hayley's latest TV documentary *The 96-year-old Schoolgirl* was broadcast on Channel 5. Filmed over three years, it followed Hayley as she went through the first drug trials in Boston and the early days at secondary school. Suddenly money started rolling into Hayley's Hope charity from the appeals we had posted on Hayley's website and her Facebook page.

With a healthy bank balance we put our differences aside and got on with the organisation. We booked the flights for all the families and set about planning days out for our guests. The first day would be an arrival day to give the families time to unwind. The second day we organised a meet and greet for all the families. Most of the families knew one another from previous events but there some new faces including Harry Crowther, an 11-year-old from Yorkshire with A-typical Progeria, and Angela from Glasgow who had lost her daughter Claire six years earlier and was attending her first reunion after finding us on Facebook. For the children we laid on face painting, arts and crafts, football games, a bouncy castle, an ice cream van, a popcorn machine and chocolate fountains. For the mums I planned an afternoon of shopping when we left the children with the dads and went off in search of bargains at the local outlet shopping centre. Mark decided he would take the dads to the Shepherd Neame Brewery for a guided tour and tasting. The Port Lympne Wild Animal Park, who had helped to make Hayley's wish come true to meet Steve Irwin all those years earlier, donated a safari day out for all the children to meet snakes and spiders and giraffes and gorillas. Another local attraction, Leeds Castle, opened its doors to us and laid on lunch and presents for the children in medieval marquees on the lawns.

The reunion was a huge success. All our progeria family friends congratulated us on making it run so smoothly. But the stress had taken its toll on Mark and me. We bravely put on a united front for our guests but behind closed doors we were fighting more than ever. There were only two levels of communication between us – raised voices or awkward silence. Throughout the week I had bitten my tongue on many occasions to prevent a full-blown public showdown. When we were alone we said the most hurtful things to one another.

'You only used me to get pregnant,' Mark shouted at me. 'Yeah and you couldn't even do that properly,' I snapped. It was well below the belt and I knew there was no going back.

The farewell party on the last night was more emotional than ever for me. Not only was I saying goodbye to all our friends, not knowing if I would ever see any of the children the following year, but my head was in the shed. I wanted out of my marriage and I had to make a decision on the future for me and the kids. Should I stay knowing I could never be happy? Or should I make the break? I struggled to put on a false smile for the final night and the next morning when Mark got up to drive one of the families to the airport, I packed our bags and fled. We didn't even have time to say goodbye. I called my mum.

'I'm leaving Mark, can you fetch us?' Mum arrived and

drove us back to their home where we stayed for two months until I could sort out the end of our relationship.

In my heart I had known for a couple of years that our relationship was going nowhere. The only thing we had really ever had in common was our love of dance and all-night raves. But with three children that life was long gone. Without it there was nothing except the children. We had grown apart. I had lots of friends and I liked going out at weekends. Mark was happy sitting in front of the computer. Where we had once bounced off one another and made each other laugh, now we just avoided one another and made each other mad. At one point I had suggested a trial separation but Mark refused, believing that once we parted we would never get back together. We had even tried counselling under the misguided notion that we should try to make things work 'for the sake of the children'. But these sessions only proved to me that we were beyond help. We were given exercises to help improve our relationship. Once we were told we had to make an effort to thank one another every time we did something good for one another. 'Thank you for putting the bins out,' I would say to Mark. To which he replied, 'Thank you for doing the washing.' It just felt unnatural and proved to me that our relationship was beyond repair. This really hit home when we were asked to list 10 good things about each other and 10 bad things. I had no trouble listing the bad things. Why stop at 10, I thought? But when it came to the good things beyond being a good dad and being good on the computer, there was nothing. On his part he said I was a good cook, a good listener and a good mother. But all these were all about practical things we did. None of us could list anything that connected to our emotions. For me it only proved what I had felt for a long time, we were totally different people.

Staying with Mum gave me the breathing space I needed to sort out my future for me and the children. Mark moved out to a new flat close to the sea and the children and I moved back into our home. Mark and I continued to share our parental responsibilities, splitting custody of the children. When it came to hospital appointments and special occasions with Hayley we laid our differences on one side and did things together. For the first time in years I was happy. I started to enjoy my own company and the atmosphere in the house improved for everyone.

One day I sat down with Hayley, Louis and Ruby and explained Mummy and Daddy were getting a divorce.

'What's a divorce?' they asked.

'When you get married you get a piece of paper to say you are married,' I explained. 'But when you are divorced that piece of paper is thrown away in the bin and you will be no longer married.'

Chapter 29
Hayley
All my Friends Have Split Parents

WHEN MUM TOLD ME her and Dad were getting divorced I felt extra sad because I had wanted them to get married in the first place. I always used to say that if two people loved each other they should get married. When they got married I could tell that Mum and Dad loved each other because they were always laughing and kissing and cuddling.

But actually now I think it's better that they are not together any more. I know it sounds a bit weird as most kids want their parents to stay together but now they aren't together they don't argue so much.

Last August before the Progeria Reunion they were so stressed they were arguing more than ever. On the last day of the reunion I was the last one to wake up. Ruby and Louis had already got up and were downstairs playing, so it was just me and Mum left together in our hotel room. Mum said to me, 'Daddy and I are going to split up.' When she told me, I was upset. I worried that I wouldn't see my dad again. I thought, what if Mum gets a horrible boyfriend or my dad gets a bad girlfriend? And that made me worry.

It was Mum's fault that I didn't get to say goodbye to my friends at the reunion. Before I had a chance to say goodbye to everyone Nanna came to pick us up and take us back to her house. When I told Mum I wanted to say goodbye to everyone she said we couldn't because we didn't have time. And I would have to see them again next year. That made me sad. I said, 'What if I don't get the chance to see them again next year?' Then Mum said 'There's things you don't know and don't need to know, but if you did know you would probably understand.' I thought that was weird and didn't make sense.

Ruby and Louis were really upset when Mum and Dad split up. As the oldest in the family I felt I had to look after them. Some nights when we were sleeping at Nanna and Pops' house Louis would cry himself to sleep. I would say to him, 'Everything is going to be all right,' and there was me actually almost crying myself because I was so upset. Ruby didn't know how to take it because she was quite young and it was harder for her to understand. Like if she was at Mum's she would be crying because she wanted Dad and if she was at Dad's she would be crying for Mum. It took a long time before she got used to them not being together.

After the first couple of weeks I started to feel happier because I noticed they were more like friends and they were laughing together again which was really good. I wished to myself that they might get back together. Then I realised 'they are not going to get back together so I have to get used to it' and it started getting better. Dad moved into a flat near the beach and now we stay two days with Mum then three days with Dad and spend the weekend with Mum. Then the next week we swap and stay with Mum in the week and the weekend with Dad. We haven't sorted it properly, but it works.

When we stay with Dad he takes us to the beach and we throw pebbles in the sea, but it's strange going without Mum being there to carry our bags and buy us ice cream. I miss our days out as a family.

I am close to my dad. I remember when I was little he used to carry me around on his shoulders and I liked being able to look over his head. Now I am older I don't like sitting on his shoulders, I'm afraid I will fall back. When I'm with my dad we laugh and joke about silly random stuff.

Dad is good at computer stuff. He runs my website. We are making a new website because the old pink one looks too young for me now that I am 13. The new one is going to be like an old photo booth with lots of pictures up the side. Dad is always taking pictures of me, Ruby and Louis. In fact he's always taking pictures of everything. Like one day there were seagulls living on top of the house opposite his flat and they had babies so he took pictures of them. Or if we are walking on the beach and he sees a really cool pebble he'll take a picture. I'm going to put lots of Dad's pictures up the side of my website.

Dad seems happier these days. He doesn't shout as much as he used to. He used to lose his temper all the time, now the only time he loses his temper is if Ruby and Louis are arguing. But when we are at Dad's house they don't even argue that much any more. It's weird because they argue all the time at Mum's. I don't get it! I think it's because they know that Dad will shout at them but Mum just grounds them. One day when we were staying at Mum's house we were arguing and we made Mum cry. I was quite shocked because she sat on her bed and cried, 'I can't do this on my own any more. You've got to help me and start being good.' Now I do try to be good but with Ruby and Louis it doesn't always work out.

At home Mum seems to treats us differently now she's not with Dad. She takes us out a lot more. Sometimes we go out to McDonald's for dinner which we never used to do when she was married to Dad. Mum is like my best friend. If we are out together and we see someone wearing a ridiculous outfit we say, 'Look at her,' and laugh. Mum is the one that takes me to Boston for my treatment too. We used to go as a family but Mum says the drugs company will only pay for one person to go with me. It's good because Ruby and Louis stay home with Dad and me and Mum get to spend some quality time together without all the arguments.

It's really weird but it's like Mum and Dad were never married and were just friends all along. It would be nice if they had stayed married but most kids I know have split parents so I'm not the only one. My best friend Erin's parents have split up, so I feel normal now.

Chapter 30
Kerry
Becoming a Teenager

AS HAYLEY'S 13TH BIRTHDAY approached we had to ignore those ominous first warnings that *'children with progeria die of heart disease or strokes at an average age of 13 years'* and assume she would pass through puberty to reach adulthood. She had such a fighting character we believed that she would be the one to beat the statistics and prove all the experts wrong. She had already marked several milestones that we once had never dared to dream of. She was taking the trial drugs to slow down the ageing process with what appeared to be positive results and her arteries and organs were in good shape. And she was attending secondary school just like any other kid – an achievement that her close friend Maddie never realised.

In spirit Hayley was already a typical teenager. She loved shopping and sleep-overs. She lived for social network sites Facebook and Twitter and had thousands of virtual friends all over the world that had seen her on TV and wanted to follow her life. And she was besotted by Canadian teen pop star Justin Bieber. Every minute of the day Hayley would be playing his hits *Baby* or *One Less Lonely Girl,* she even had life-sized posters on her bedroom wall. Whenever his name was mentioned I would tease her by saying, 'You love him,' and she would blush.

As the actual date of her 13th birthday approached, my initial excitement of her reaching her teens was replaced with a fear. I was afraid to tempt fate by going over the top to mark her birthday, yet I wanted to make it special.

From a very early age we had started a tradition of treating every birthday as if it might be her last. For her first couple of birthday we had the tea parties for close family. For her fourth birthday we took her bowling with her Nanna and Pops and auntie Janie. Her fifth birthday was extra special as it coincided with her Child of Courage Award in London. And for several years after we combined her birthday celebrations with return invitations to the awards ceremonies in London. But as the years passed Mark and I became aware of the need to fulfil as many of her childhood dreams as we could. 'She will never have the opportunity to see the world when she's our age, so we have to take her together and share the experience.'

Swimming with dolphins was high on her wish list after watching dolphins perform at one of the marine theme parks when we were on holiday in Florida. The TV programme *This Morning* had heard about this and for her eighth birthday they arranged to fly the family to Marineland park in the south of France. To add to the surprise the tickets were handed to her by Crocodile Hunter Steve Irwin when they met at the zoo.

On the morning of the trip I was forced to stay home with sickness so Mark took her. As they boarded the plane at Stansted airport, the pilot announced 'We have to wish a happy eighth birthday to a special young lady. Hayley Okines is going to swim with dolphins.' Then Hayley's big blue eyes lit up when a flight attendant appeared with a big pink birthday cake and everyone on board joined in a chorus of Happy Birthday.

At the marine park Hayley was taken to the dolphin

pool to live out her dream. She was too frail to risk actually swimming with the dolphins but they gave her a special swimming costume and extra-long waders so that she could walk into the pool and stroke the animals. The trainer showed her how to make them sing and as she waggled her bony fingers in the air they sang happy birthday in their squeaky dolphin voices. The whole trip was filmed and later broadcast on the prime time TV show *This Morning*, so even though I couldn't be there on the day I was able to relive her dream with her. As we sat down together at home to watch the programme the S Club 7 hit 'Never Had A Dream Come True' was played out as the soundtrack and Hayley turned to me and said, 'This is our song Mum.' I almost cried knowing that she had experienced something that most children of her age could only dream of. To this day, whenever I hear that song, it brings a lump to my throat.

For her ninth birthday we took her to see the pyramids in Egypt. Like many children of that age she was fascinated by the idea of mummies and wanted to know where they lived, so we had promised to take her. On the morning of her birthday the family woke up in a hotel room looking out over the pyramids at Giza. Mark and Louis rode a camel up to the pyramids but I was worried that a camel ride might be too bumpy for Hayley's ageing bones, so I took the girls on a horse and cart ride across the sand dunes. When we arrived at the great pyramid, we found ourselves surrounded by curious Egyptian children. But it wasn't Hayley they were interested in for a change – it was Ruby. She was only 18 months old and had a shock of white/blonde hair and blue eyes so dark-skinned Egyptian children were fascinated by her colouring and wanted to take photographs.

When she turned 12 Hayley finally got the opportunity

to swim with dolphins when the make-a-wish charity The Starlight Foundation arranged for the family to fly out to Discovery Cove in Florida. As she was older and slightly taller than when she had her previous marine encounter, Hayley was allowed to get in the pool along with Louis. She giggled as she held onto the dolphins' fins and they dragged her though the water.

As she neared her 13th birthday, the childish thrill of swimming with dolphins was replaced by a new dream – meeting her favourite pop star, Justin Bieber. It was a tall order and one that I wasn't sure I would be able to achieve. After all we were talking about one of the biggest pop stars in the world. Even trying to find an email or contact for his management was impossible.

Then a couple of weeks before her birthday I got a phone call from Hawaii.

'Hi, my name is Scooter Braun, Justin Bieber's management company. I hear that your little girl Hayley wants to meet Justin Bieber.'

At first I thought it was a joke and thinking back I was probably rather ruder than I should have been with my non-committal, 'Yeah, that's right,' reply. But I really thought I was being stitched up as part of some sick hoax.

The voice on the other end of the phone continued, 'Justin's in London next week doing some TV and radio promotion. If you can get to London we can fix it up.'

OMG! It was no hoax. It was real. Justin's manager explained how they had been alerted to Hayley's wish on Twitter.

Hayley had been Tweeting about her Bieber Fever and a group of girls in America and the UK, who were following her on Twitter, had taken it upon themselves to make her dream happen. They had set up a hashtag #BiebsmeetHayley. Not being part of the Twitter generation I didn't really understand how these things worked. But it appeared that Hayley's friends had created a plea to Justin Bieber begging him to make her dream come true. This message went viral spreading from the original five girls via their followers and their followers' followers until it became so huge that it was one of the 'trending' most popular topics all over the global site and the girls who started it all made the news in America. That's when Justin Bieber's managers heard about it and tracked us down via Hayley's website.

I couldn't begin to imagine how excited Hayley would be. It was the kind of present no money could buy. She was going to meet the hottest teen pin-up in the world? If anyone had told me that I would meet George Michael or the guy from the Levi jeans commercial when I was 13 I would have burst. I knew it was going to make Hayley's day. All I had to do was get her to London without raising any suspicion.

Chapter 31
Hayley
I Felt Sooo Lucky to Be Alive

I WAS REALLY EXCITED because I was going to be a teenager. My drugs were working and making me live longer. I thought that when I was 13 I would be grown up and my mum would have to let me go to the shops on my own with my friends. Usually she doesn't like me going out without her, she worries something will happen to me.

When Mum asked me what I wanted to do for my birthday, I said meet Justin Bieber. That would have been the best present in the world. But I knew I probably couldn't have that so instead I said I would have a sleep-over. I like having sleep-overs. Usually Ruby and Louis go to stay with Dad when my friends sleep over. We have dinner, and then play on my Wii games and watch DVDs. Usually if it's just my friend Erin we sleep in my bedroom. If I have two or three friends we pile up the duvets and pillows in the dining room and sleep there. I always sleep on the sofa because it's comfier for me. We get to stay up really late, until the early hours of the morning sometimes, just talking. If it's really late Mum texts me and says go to sleep. For my birthday Mum said that I could ask my friend Jessica, who is really funny, to sleep over with my cousin Sophie, who is 10, and her friend who is also called Jessica.

I have been lucky, I have had some really cool birthdays. Once I went to France to swim with dolphins. I don't remember a lot about it except that the water was cold and we played soccer with them. I have a video of me with the dolphins which is funny to watch because I looked so little. Another year I remember going to the pyramids in Egypt and there were lots of kids gathering around Ruby because she was so little. I was glad they weren't all looking at me because I would have been scared. For my 12th birthday we went to see the dolphins in Discovery Cove in Orlando and it was really nice. We had a private little bit with drinks and stuff that was fun. In France I stood in the pool but in Orlando we got right in with the dolphins and held on to their fins while I swam. I had to wear two wet suits so I wouldn't get cold. I held on to the dolphin's fin and it dragged me through the water. It was quite scary as I almost slipped off and the water was quite deep and I wasn't wearing a life jacket.

I hoped that for my 13th birthday maybe Mum might be planning a surprise party for me as well as the sleep-over. Mum is not usually good at surprises. I remember one year when I was four or five she picked me up from school on my birthday and told me she had a surprise for me. I said 'Am I going bowling?' She asked me how I guessed. I said that I heard her talking to someone on the phone. Mum was disappointed that I found out but I said, 'We can still go bowling; it just won't be a surprise.' That was the same year that Mum and Dad bought me a costume like Tinkerbell the fairy and I wanted to wear it bowling because I thought I looked gorgeous, but Mum wouldn't let me. When we got to the bowling alley Nanna and Pops were waiting with my Auntie Janie and my cousins Sophie and Jack and they all said surprise. I didn't know they were coming so it was a bit of a surprise after all.

One day before my 13th birthday I overheard Mum talking on the phone to someone called Alison. She was talking about meeting somewhere, but I couldn't hear what she was talking about. When I asked her who she was talking to, she said, 'just a friend'. I thought that was suspicious as she usually tells me the names of her friends. I thought it might be Alison Hammond, who we had been watching on the TV programme *I'm A Celebrity Get Me Out Of Here*. She was also on the TV show *This Morning* and was there when I met Steve Irwin for my birthday so I thought that maybe Mum was planning a surprise party for my 13th birthday. She said we were going to go shopping in London for my birthday. I have been to London lots for hospitals and when I am interviewed on TV but I had never been shopping before. I didn't know what sort of shops they had there, so I said it would be cool.

I was on Facebook the day before my birthday and I had some messages from my friends Emily, Charlie, Lauren, Casey and Sydney. They had made a video and posted it on YouTube. It said: 'December 3 1997, the most precious little girl was born. She goes by the name of Hayley Okines. This girl is a pocketful of sunshine. She's so sweet, so kind, so loving, so caring, and so full of smiles and so many other incredible things. You've grown so much from a young baby to a young adult. Happy 13th birthday Hayley. We all hope you have the best birthday ever. We hope you live plenty more years filled with health, happiness, smiles, laughter, friends and family. We love you so much from all the girls in BiebsmeetHayley.' On the video loads of girls who were my friends held up cards and said happy birthday. It was so sweet. I had never met Emily, Charlie, Lauren, Casey and Sydney before but they had seen me on telly and asked to be my friend on Facebook.

185

Lots of my friends love Justin Bieber and when I said I would love to meet him they put it on Twitter. It said 'Justin, Hayley is fighting for her life. It's her dying wish to meet you, please help make it come true. We love you Hayley.' #BiebsmeetHayley. Loads of people Tweeted it around the world and it got so big that the girls got to be on TV in America.

I have liked Justin Bieber for ages. I first heard him when I was round my friend Lydia's house and she was listening to him. I thought, who's this? And she showed me his video on YouTube. He was really fit. Then I got a bit obsessed and started playing his music all the time on YouTube. I cut out his pictures and stuck them on my bedroom wall. Lydia bought me a giant poster for my birthday which is like almost as big as real life. Last Christmas Mum bought me a Justin Bieber calendar. I had it on my bedroom wall until Ruby started kissing it, which is so annoying because she was never bothered about him till I started liking him. Mum had to move it where she can't reach it. I can't reach it either but I don't want to kiss it all the time like her. My friends on Facebook like him too. We always talk about what it would be like to meet him and what we would do. I think that maybe I am his biggest fan.

I hoped that one day I could meet Justin Bieber. My friends in America said they hoped that one day they can meet me which is really sweet. I have asked my mum if we can make it happen and she says 'We'll see.' It makes me happy when everyone says nice things about me!

On the day of my actual birthday I had lots of cards and presents and £110 in money. Mum took me shopping in the morning. We bought cake and crisps and chocolate for my sleep-over. The next morning after the sleep-over, my friends went home and me, Mum, Dad, Ruby and Louis and my cousin Sophie went up to London shopping.

When we got there Mum took us into this really posh hotel. I asked her why we were going there. She hesitated and said we were going to get coffee because it was cold outside. I said to my cousin Sophie that doesn't sound right. It was weird because I am always the one that gets cold and I always have to wear a cardigan even in the summer because I have progeria and I don't have much body fat to keep me warm like other kids. Anyway we went into the hotel and I took off my gloves and hat. I said I wanted to go to the toilet so me and Sophie went to the toilet. While we were in the toilet Sophie said to me, 'What would you do if Justin Bieber was here?' 'I would scream,' I said. When I came back I heard Mum on the phone to that woman called Alison again. I thought it must be the one from *This Morning*. Mum told us to go upstairs and wait for her. So we did. When we came back Justin Bieber was standing there. I thought, that's not possible. It can't be Justin Bieber. But it really was. I tried to play it cool but I screamed and ran towards him and hugged him. My arms only reached his waist because he was really tall. But he put his arm around me and I kept thinking, I am the luckiest girl in the world. Justin Bieber is holding me! We sat down next to each other and we talked about my friends and my progeria and how cool it was to meet him. Then he asked what I wanted for Christmas and I said, 'You!' and he laughed and I went a bit red. Then he said he was going to be on *X Factor* the next night and asked if I watched *X Factor*. I said I would definitely watch it if he was on. And he laughed. He said he was coming back to Britain to do a concert in a couple of months and would I like to have front-row seats. I just said, 'Yes please!' I thought, it can't get any better than this. My life is complete.

Before Justin left Mum got her camera out and asked if

we could take a picture. He put his arm around me and smiled and I smiled back my biggest smile ever. My favourite song of Justin's is *U Smile*. In it he sings, 'When you smile, I smile.' I thought this is true it's really happening.

When we were going home I said to Sophie, 'Did you know we were going to meet Justin Bieber?' She said she didn't and I believed her.

When I got home I went on Facebook and said I had met him. All my friends like him even more now. They say he is a caring person. Even Mum said he was lovely and normally she only likes men with big guns – that's what she calls muscles. Meeting Justin Bieber was definitely the best day of my life ever!

I didn't think it could get any better but then three months later on March 17 2011 we went to see him in concert in London with the front-row seats he had promised and I got to meet him again. I went with Mum, Erin, Auntie Janie and my cousin Sophie. Before Justin came on stage we saw Willow Smith. She is like only eleven and is a really big pop star. Her dad is the famous movie star Will Smith. When she was on stage she saw me in the front row dancing and waving and she waved back. When she finished singing one of the bodyguards came up to Mum and said Willow would like to meet me back stage. I thought that was really cool. We went back stage and everyone was looking at us thinking, who are they? Why are they going back stage? I felt really special.

Back stage Willow came out of her dressing room to say hello. She was really wicked. I said I thought she was a really good singer and she asked if I would have my photo taken with her like I was the famous person not her. Then she asked for my address and gave me her email and told me to email her anytime.

Then who should come along but Justin Bieber. He was even nicer than I remembered the first time. And he actually remembered me and thanked me for coming. I said it was OK, he didn't have to thank me. I felt good to think that he sees loads of girls all over the world but he remembered who I was. Mum asked if he would do a video for my new website. He looked at the camera and said, 'Hi. Welcome to Hayley's new website.' That is so cool I can't wait until Dad gets time to put it on my new website. How many girls can say Justin Bieber has given them a special message? Then I thought how many girls can say they have met Justin Bieber – twice! I felt sooo lucky to be alive.

Chapter 32
Kerry
The Future

AS I HAVE SAID many times, I believe that Hayley will be the one child to prove the experts wrong, and so far I seem to be right. She has grown into a stroppy teenager with a stinking attitude to match. Like many girls her age she thinks she has a God-given right to leave all her books and clothes strewn across her bedroom and, when I ask her to do something, she constantly mutters under her breath. I should get annoyed with her, but I just feel relief that she is a normal thirteen-year-old. She has even reached puberty, something we were originally told would be unlikely to happen.

Whenever I look at Hayley and see how happy and well-adjusted she is it, I am always reminded of those early days when I wanted to take both our lives. Now I am so glad I never carried out my plan. I would have robbed her of an extraordinary and long life. Hayley would never have made the good friends she has or met all the famous people and other special children.

Having a child with a terminal illness has made me a stronger person. There was a time when I couldn't talk about death without bursting into tears, but now I appreciate life and family. I never take it for granted that

191

my family will always be there and I have learnt to enjoy life and appreciate people, especially my mum, while I can. That's not to say I don't have my moments. There are times when all the children are in school and I am sitting alone in the house and I try to imagine what life would be like without Hayley, not being able to see her sitting on the sofa, or her iPad left on the chair. Then I think of the wise words of a friend who lost her daughter to progeria when she was fifteen: 'Don't waste your time grieving for Hayley when she is here. Make every day count.' And I soon snap out of the negative thoughts and get on with life.

No matter how much I try to protect Hayley in our daily life, there are some things on the internet that are beyond my control. Just the other day my brother called and I could tell by his voice he was upset.

'Are you OK?' he asked. 'Yeah we're all fine,' I replied and immediately I could sense a change in his voice.

'I just saw on the internet that Hayley had died.' I reassured him that everything was fine but I could tell he had been shaken. When I put the phone down, I Googled Hayley's name and sure enough there were thousands of people writing on their blogs and websites that Hayley had died. It didn't bother me that these rumours were spreading, because I knew they were lies, but it shook my brother who believed what he had read. I sat down and wrote, 'I am Hayley's mum and Hayley is running around in the garden perfectly fine,' hoping to put an end to the Chinese whisper. When Hayley found out about the rumour she just shrugged her shoulders and said, 'That's OK, I've read that Justin Bieber has died six times.'

At times I have to monitor the message board on Hayley's website to filter out any nasty comments. Although the internet has been responsible for many good things in Hayley's life, like the meeting with Justin Bieber and the fund-raising for the UK Progeria reunion, it can also bring some ignorant and hurtful comments like, 'Why has that girl got a bald head?' or 'That girl looks so weird.' It's quite normal for Hayley to get up to one thousand messages a month, sometimes even more if one of her documentary programmes has been shown somewhere in the world, and the majority of comments on her page are always positive and talk of Hayley being a 'ray of sunshine' or a 'true inspiration' but it's hard for me to ignore the nasty ones, which I see as a form of cyber-bullying. Recently a boy posted a message on my Facebook page: 'Your child looks like an alien and I'm an alien mother from space. I'm going to come down and take my baby.' I wrote back: 'You pathetic boy, take a good look at yourself in the mirror before you criticise other people.'

The drug trials have been a great help in keeping our hopes alive. We are still waiting for official results from the first FTI trial, which are four years overdue, but so far there is nothing. We continue to allow Hayley and other children to be treated like guinea pigs without having definite answers. But what choice do we have? Without the drugs we all know what the prognosis is. I take heart from the fact that since the trials started I have not heard of one child who has passed away whereas in the past at least one to five children would pass away each year. We're also encouraged by what we see with our own eyes. We don't need doctors to tell us that Hayley is looking healthier. Instead of shrivelling like some of the wizened children we used to see on the internet, she is flourishing. Her facial features have filled out; she has gained weight and has moved up to an age 5 in clothing. Her blue eyes sparkle brighter than ever.

The research into a cure is speeding ahead. The second trial is coming to an end and in 2012 we will take part in a third trial. We have not been given any official confirmation of what this trial will be but recently there have been news reports about a drug which the media has called the 'forever young' drug that could make us all live 10 years longer. I hadn't connected this drug with Hayley's progeria trials until I got a call from a journalist asking what I thought about this new 'elixir of life' drug Rapamycin. When I checked it out on the Progeria Research Foundation website I discovered that the scientists in Boston had published the findings of their latest experiment. Using the progeria cells and tissues taken from Hayley and some of the other children at earlier trials they had been testing this drug and discovered that it 'flushed out' the defective protein from the progeria cells making them healthy again and extending their life. The drug had also been given to mice and found that they were living a third longer.

It's incredible to think that Hayley, Michiel and others like them could be paving the way for generations to live longer and healthier lives. But on a purely selfish note I hope it will extend Hayley's own life even further. Like all good things Rapamycin has a downside – there are higher risks. The drug was originally found in bacteria in soil samples from Easter Island in the 1960s and is currently given to transplant patients to stop them rejecting their donor organs. Some of the side-effects are that it increases cholesterol levels in patients and suppresses their immune system, making them more vulnerable to infections. I am not overly concerned as Hayley has always had a reasonably strong immune system. Apart from a few throat infections when she was a baby, she has never suffered from any infections or bugs like her brother and sister. I think all the drugs she takes actually make her stronger. And we know that her cholesterol level is in check because of our regular check-ups with Dr Whincup, so we are hoping Hayley will be able to withstand any adverse effects. Dr Gordon at the PRF has told us they are waiting for the go-ahead to use a modified version of Rapamycin that has fewer side-effects, so once they get the approval we'll be off to Boston again.

We are still struggling financially, but we manage. Mark is job-hunting and although I am officially Hayley's full-time carer, money is tight. I am always amazed by the generosity and good will of strangers who send cheques to Hayley's Fund. Her website even has a PayPal link, where people who have heard of Hayley's condition through her TV documentaries or various media interviews can make donations if they wish. That money helps to pay for her days out and special holidays. We also have a PO Box and it is quite normal to open it and find anonymous cash gifts or gifts for Hayley. Bandanas are a common item. Initially we would thank everyone personally but over the years it has become impossible to answer all the well-wishers. Since the separation I have resigned as vice-chairman of Hayley's Hope charity but Mark's daughter Charlotte now fills the role. Once again the charity is organising another Progeria Reunion in the UK at the end of October and many of the donations go towards this. Fortunately the Progeria Research Foundation continue to fund the travel for Hayley and me to visit America regularly, but if there ever came a time when they could no longer afford it I would happily take out a bank loan and run up a debt to ensure Hayley gets the best treatment available.

No longer do we live for each day like it was Hayley's last, we are planning ahead. Soon she will be 14 and I want her to have success and ambition. For years she has nagged me to buy her a puppy and in the past I have resisted thinking it would be too boisterous but last year for Christmas we bought her a Shih Tzu puppy which she named Angel. Angel follows her everywhere. She is also talking about going to college in Eastbourne or Hastings to study hairdressing and beauty with the idea of opening her own salon. She has also started talking about learning to drive and what car she would like. I have three years to save up for driving lessons because I know in my heart she will get behind the steering wheel and I can't wait to watch her take her first kangaroo jumps along our road in her instructor's car. I also need to give her more freedom. Like all teenage girls, Hayley loves shopping and wants her independence to shop with her friends. I drive her to the shopping centre and wait outside in the car while she and her friends shop or I allow her to go to her friend Erin's house. She always carries her phone on her and knows I am never more than a call away.

My biggest fear is that when her time comes I am not going to be there. I try not to think about it but I can't help myself. It's the last thing on my mind when I go to sleep at night and the first thing I think of when I wake up in the morning. If she is upstairs in her bedroom reading quietly, I shout up the stairs, 'Are you all right?' and she always replies with a bored, 'Yes, Mum.' Or if I hear a bang, where she has dropped her book on the floor, I fly up the stairs expecting the worst. I try to hide my fears from her most times.

I truly believe there is life after death and that has helped me through the tough times. I belong to the spiritualist church and one evening as I was leaving the house for a church meeting, Hayley asked, 'Do you believe in angels and fairies, Mum?'

'Of course I do. You're my little angel, aren't you?' I replied trying to keep emotion from my voice.

'I know that Maddie is an angel in heaven. And one day I will be an angel too. When I am an angel I will sit on your back and blow in your ear,' she said.

I take strength from the belief that whatever the future holds, Hayley will always be my angel.

Chapter 33
Hayley
Eighteen for Ever

MY ONE BIG WISH is to have my eighteenth birthday and stay eighteen for ever. I think it would be cool to be eighteen because I will be old enough to drive and I can get a job and have a house.

Me and Erin have our futures all figured out. We are going to own a hair and beauty salon together and live in a really big house. Erin says we should go to New York and live in Grand Central Station but I would like to live in Hawaii because I've heard that it's really hot and sunny there and it seems really nice.

If I can't live in Hawaii then I would like to live near my Nanna. On the way to Nanna's house there's a big wooden house for sale. I don't know how much it is but I want to save up enough money to buy it. I will have a big Jacuzzi bath and flat-screen TVs in every room and Nanna and Pops and Mum and Dad can come and stay with me. Ruby and Louis can come too as long as they promise to be good and not fight. I also want to have another dog to keep my dog Angel company. Maybe a Chihuahua or a Yorkshire terrier because they are small and cute and I can dress them up in bootees. I want a husky too because I love their eyes, they are blue like mine.

When I leave school I want to learn to drive and I want

a Mini Cooper or a VW Beetle in pink. When I was out shopping with Mum the other day she pointed to a small car called a Smart car that looked like a bubble and said that's what I should have. I said, 'No way. It's not cool enough. I want a Mini.' I would like my Mini to be a convertible so I can drive down to the beach in the summer with my friends, roof down and music on my iPod. I am a little bit worried about how I will be able to drive if I sit in the driver's seat and my feet can't reach the pedals. But Mum says I can have a special automatic car with controls on the steering wheel instead of pedals, which would be really cool.

I think that maybe when I grow up I will get married. But I'm not sure if I want to have children. Ruby and Louis have definitely put me off. I don't have a boyfriend and I'm not interested in boys at the moment. Mum says it will have to be someone very special to see beyond my progeria.

The drug trials have been going OK. I have grown a little bit and have put on a bit of weight. Everything looks all right. When the doctors smile it usually means it's good. Next year Mum and I will be going back to Boston for our third drug trial. There is a new drug called Rapamycin which they say cleans the cells of progeria and can make you live longer. They have said it will be another tablet that I can take with the FTI, bisphosphonate and statin to help me live longer. The woman at the Boston Hospital said to Mum she could not tell her the name of the new drug. But then we read stories on the internet that it was called the 'forever young' drug which they reckon can extend human life for everyone up to 10 years. They are experimenting on progeria children like me. It's good news because if this drug works I could live longer but there is talk that it could be used for everyone. It's been called the 'elixir of youth' which sounds like something from a space movie. I'm really excited because what we are doing could change things for everyone in the world not just a couple of hundred progeria children which is really cool. In some ways I feel less like a guinea pig because the new drug is not just for us progeria kids but for everyone. But I also feel more like a guinea pig because we are the ones who are going to be taking it to see if it works. They have only tested the drug on mice so far, so I would be the first person to take it which is quite scary. But it's really cool when I think that everyone, even Mum and Dad and Nanna and Pops, could live longer because of a drug I am taking.

Because of the drug trials I feel like I have a future to plan. I feel taller and I'm growing lots of hair. I am also getting bigger; I used to wear age 2–3 clothes before I started the trials now I am wearing age 4–5. The other day Mum bought me new trousers for school and they were age 6.

And to all the doctors and people who said there was no hope for children with progeria and they don't live long I want to say, 'You're wrong.'

**Find out more about the extraordinary
life of Hayley Okines**

Follow Hayley's blog @ hayleyokines.wordpress.com

 facebook.com/OldBeforeMyTime

 @ProgeriaBook

**To donate to Hayley's Fund,
please visit Hayley's Progeria Page**

http://hayleyspage.com

Sign up for Hayley's newsletter by scanning the QR code

202